Eleonora's Amazing Eats

The essence of Eleonora comes to you
through her intentionally incomplete
and everlasting labors of love.

May you enjoy embellishing and perhaps
completing some of her recipes.

Contributions to recipes, images, and various content by:

Eleonora's Sister
   Angelina Annunziata Moccia Barcello

Eleonora's Children
   Dominick Watson
   Martha Nuzzo DiBiccari
   Thomas Watson

Eleonora's Grandchildren
   Joyce Nuzzo Taborsak
   Brian Watson
   Greg Watson
   Renee Watson

Eleonora's Extended Family
   Camille Watson, daughter-in-law
   Ann Marie Barcello Ladrigan, niece
   Theresa Barcello Metzgar, niece
   Michael Barcello, nephew
   Regina Barcello, niece

Dedication

To the incredible Eleonora:
Our Artist in the Kitchen and Heart of our Family
Cherished by all, you will forever bring loved ones together.

Acknowledgments

To the many family and friends of Eleonora, who penned
her recipes and provided their unique knowledge of her
and her efforts in the kitchen.
Thank you.

Mangia!

From my kitchen to yours...
with love,

Eleonora Watson

Content

Introduction to Eleonora
Artist in the Kitchen & Heart of our Family

Elinor. Eleanor. Eleonor. There are many spellings of her name over the past century. Regardless of how it was spelled, she remained true to her Italian food-influenced heritage.

Named Eleonora Moccia, she was born in San Mango Sul Calore, Italy, to Domenico Moccia and Domenica Prizio-Moccia on February 13, 1916. A mere nineteen days later, on March 3, her mother passed away of complications. Her father, even as a single parent with a newborn, was drafted into the Italian Army during World War I (1916 & 1922). After his first tour of duty, Domenico returned and married Concetta Coppola, perhaps as a means to regain custody of his daughter. In 1920, their family grew and Eleonora became a big sister to a baby brother named Tommas.

In June of 1928, Eleonora, Tommas, and Concetta emigrated to the United States on the steamship Christoper Columbus. Domenico followed later and eventually the family settled in Stamford, Connecticut. The Moccia family continued to grow and over the next six years Eleonora was blessed with more siblings. Angelina Annunziata (Annunciation) was born on March, 25, 1929, and Theresa was born on October 28, 1932. Unfortunate circumstances arose in May 1935, which pushed Eleonora into the role of surrogate mom to her three younger siblings.

It was the Great Depression. Domenico was fortunate to work as a laborer building roads and bridges for the Works Progress Administration (WPA) in Stamford, Connecticut under President Theodore Roosevelt's American New Deal agency. The tough times trickled into the kitchen. The daily struggle to amass ample, and satisfying, food to please family of five would challenge any adult, not to mention a teen. It seems this was the start of Eleonora's metamorphosis from typical teenager into artist in the kitchen.

The Moccia family, Eleonora, Concetta Coppoloa-Moccia, Tommas, and Domenico Moccia prior to Domenico's second tour of duty in the Italian Army in 1922.

Family stories indicate that photographers spliced Domenico into this image at a later date.

Emigration paperwork, 1928.

Eleonora with Dominick, Martha, and the garden in Stamford, circa 1946.

On July 2, 1939, Eleonora married Angelo Piccini and they welcomed their first child, Dominick, in April 1940. Despite the interruptions of World War II service duties, Eleonora and Angelo, who later changed his name to Paul Watson (another story), welcomed Martha and Thomas to their family. Through it all, Eleonora continued her surrogate mother duties to her siblings until they were successfully married (Tommas 1945, Angelina 1949, and Theresa 1950) and started their own households. Opportunities remained limited in the 1940s and 1950s, the family lived a close-knit life in a tiny apartment on Wright Street in Stamford, Connecticut.

Even in modest city surroundings, Eleonora kept an incredible garden, which yielded an abundance of vegetables – and every edible morsel was eaten. With loads of fresh produce, Eleonora's kitchen was often filled with her family and friends. Everyone easily overlooked the cramped quarters to enjoy her amazing eats or a session of canning.

A true master at keeping family close, Eleonora intentionally never wrote out a complete recipe and rarely recounted the full ingredients or steps for anyone. Captured in the following pages are the heroic efforts of family and friends to pen and preserve recipes of Eleonora's through the years. It seems this effort could very well endure time. At this time, we welcome readers, recipe-lovers, and story-aficionados to help recreate and possibly complete some of Eleonora's artistry in the kitchen.

We hope you enjoy being part of our effort!

The Entrées, Appetizers, & Extras

Aioli Anchovy & Pasta

Brian Watson

¼ cup fine diced onions (optional)
1 clove garlic
2-3 cans of anchovies
1 cup starchy pasta water
Olive oil
Pepper, basil, oregano, and garlic to taste
Pasta of choice. Linguine or spaghetti is recommended.

1. Sauté onions and garlic in oil.
2. Add anchovies and cook for 5 to 10 minutes.
3. Add seasonings.
4. Add oil as needed.
5. Add starchy pasta water, approximately 1 cup.
6. Reduce.
7. Serve over cooked pasta of choice.

Notes:

_____

_____

_____

_____

_____

_____

_____

_____

_____

_____

_____

_____

Braciole

Camille Watson

Beef, sliced (top round, flank, or skirt steak preferred)
Prosciutto
Parmesan cheese
Bread crumbs, Italian-style
Garlic, chopped
Parsley, preferably fresh
Olive oil

1. Pound steaks to tenderize and butterfly cut the thickness of the meat in half.
2. Top each section with a slice of prosciutto.
3. Combine cheese, bread crumbs, garlic and parsley, then sprinkle over each. Tuck in sides to secure filing and roll into cylinders. Secure with a toothpick.
4. Brown in olive oil. Let sit to set-up well.
5. Simmer in wine-infused pasta sauce until tender, preferably several hours.

Best served with penne, rigatoni, or ziti.

Notes:

Bread

Brian Watson

6 cups flour
4 envelopes active dry yeast
5 tablespoons sugar
4 tablespoons salt
6 tablespoons olive oil
2¾ cups water at 100° F to 110° F

1. Add yeast and warm water in a bowl. Let bloom for at least 15 minutes.
2. Add salt, flour, oil, and water-yeast mixture to large bowl and combine.
3. Knead on a floured surface until smooth and elastic, about 6 to 8 minutes.
4. Add additional flour as needed.
5. Put in an oiled bowl. Cover with plastic wrap and towels and let rise for at least 90 minutes.
6. Divide in half and put in 2 oiled loaf pans and let rise again for 60 minutes.
7. Bake at 400° F for approximately 20 to 25 minutes or until lightly golden brown.

Makes 2 9-inch loaves.

Ann Marie notes, after a wedding the women would return to Eleonor's apartment and make bread fresh for the bride and groom saying it was an important Italian tradition.

Notes:

_____

_____

_____

_____

_____

_____

_____

_____

_____

_____

_____

Broccoli Cheese Bake

1 unbaked pie shell
1 package frozen chopped broccoli, cooked, and drained
1 10 ¾-ounce can condensed cheddar cheese soup
1 cup shredded sharp cheddar cheese
1 egg, well beaten
1 can mushrooms, chopped
1 cup chicken, cooked and diced (optional)
¼ cup cornflakes, crumbled
¼ cup slivered almonds

1. If frozen, thaw pie shell for 20 minutes.
2. Mix broccoli, soup, egg, cheese, mushrooms, and chicken.
3. Pour into pie crust.
4. Sprinkle cornflakes and almonds on top.
5. Bake at 350° F for 30 to 35 minutes.

Serves 6

Eleonora's Amazing Eats

Cavatelli

Ann Marie Barcello Ladrigan

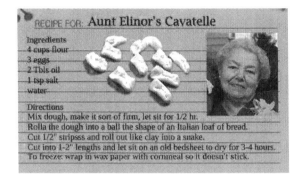

RECIPE FOR: **Aunt Elinor's Cavatelle**

Ingredients
4 cups flour
3 eggs
2 Tbls oil
1 tsp salt
water

Directions
Mix dough, make it sort of firm, let sit for 1/2 hr.
Rolla the dough into a ball the shape of an Italian loaf of bread.
Cut 1/2" stripsss and roll out like clay into a snake.
Cut into 1-2" lengths and let sit on an old bedsheet to dry for 3-4 hours.
To freeze: wrap in wax paper with cornmeal so it doesn't stick.

4 cups flour
3 eggs
2 Tablespoons oil
1 teaspoon salt
Water

1. Mix ingredients, added water until the dough is "sort of" firm.
2. Let dough sit for about 30 minutes.
3. Form dough into the shape of an Italian-style loaf bread.
4. Cut into ½-inch strips and roll out "like a clay snake."
5. Cut into 1-inch lengths. Let sit on an old bed sheet or thin cotton fabric to dry, about 3 hours.
6. Now, "press and pull." Using tips of index and middle fingers, firmly press each piece while pulling toward you. The dough lengthens slightly and forms a curl in the middle.
7. Transfer cavatelli to baking sheets. Repeat with remaining dough.
8. Boil until al dente.

To freeze, wrap in wax paper with cornmeal to avoid sticking.
Does not require defrosting before cooking.

"The secrets as they were given and ordered never to write down."
~Ann Marie Barcello Ladrigan

Notes:

Easter Macaroni Pie

Dominick and Brian Watson

1 pound macaroni, size of elbows to small penne
6 eggs
Sausage, loosely packed or removed from casings
Grated cheese
Black pepper
½ pound butter
2 cups of starchy pasta water

1. Cook macaroni. Be careful to not overcook.
2. Save 2 cups of starchy pasta water.
3. Drain macaroni, return to pot and add about 1 to 2 cups of starchy water.
4. In bowl, scramble eggs, season with some grated cheese, and black pepper.
5. While in pot, mix butter in macaroni and season with pepper and cheese.
6. Turn off the burner and stir.
7. Mix in eggs. Make sure it is wet/juicy.
8. Put mixture in baking pan(s).
9. Bake at 375° F until brown, about 30 to 45 minutes.

Notes:

_____
_____
_____
_____
_____
_____
_____
_____
_____
_____
_____
_____

Macaroni Pie was a popular
Easter dish of Eleonora's

Easter Pie: Pizza Chiena

Ann Marie Barcello Ladrigan

<u>Dough:</u>
6 eggs
8 cups flour
3 heaping teaspoons baking powder
Water
Cream cheese (optional)

<u>Filling:</u>
2 pounds ham cubed
2 pounds sausage browned, loosely packaged or removed from casing
3 pounds farmer's cheese in baskets, drained
2 pounds ricotta cheese, drained
6-8 hard boiled eggs, mashed
6-8 fresh eggs
1 can grated cheese
Prosciutto (optional)

1. Mix dough together the day before. Let sit in refrigerator.
2. Roll out and place in well greased pie pan.
3. Mix together ham, sausage, farmer's cheese, ricotta, mashed hardboiled eggs, and prosciutto (optional).
4. Add fresh eggs and grated cheese to mixture. Combine to make a thick consistency.
5. Pour into pie crust.
6. Glaze top with beaten egg yolk.
7. While cooking, mop up any juice that comes out on top.
8. Pinch or snip the top of crust with scissors.
9. Bake at 350° F for 45 minutes.
10. Remove from dish and place on sheet to cool.

Angie's Italian Lesson:
Pizza Gana, is actually "Pizza Chiena" which translates to Filled Pizza. Also, the "real" Italian term is "Pizza Piena" - Chiena is an Italian dialect word for "full or filled."

RECIPE FOR: Pizza Gana (Easter Pie)
350° Bake   45 min.   Aunt Eleanor
Dough
6 eggs   water
8 cups flour   cream cheese (optional)
3 heaping tsp. baking powder
        Mix the day before, let sit in fridge, then roll out.
        Grease pie pan well.

Pie   lbs in
2 lbs. ham cubed   3 baskets drained farmer cheese
2 lbs. sausage browned   2 lbs drained ricotta
        (take out of casing)
bruscuitto (optional)   6-8 hard boiled eggs (mashed)
1 can grated cheese *   * 6-8 fresh eggs
        Mix together everything except *, then add * to make
thick consistency.
        Pour into pie crust. Glaze top w/ beaten egg yolk. While
Cooking mop up any juice that comes out on top. Pinch top
of crust w/ scissors. When done take out of dish & place

Easter Pie: Pizza Rustica

Dominick Watson

Crust:
1 package yeast
¼ cup warm water
2 cups flour
½ cup butter
2 eggs, 1 for crust and 1 for wash

Filling:
1½ pounds ricotta
½ pound mozzarella, shredded
1 pound prosciutto, chopped
1 pound fresh cheese or farmer's cheese, diced*
5 eggs, hard boiled, chopped to mix
5 fresh eggs
½ cup grated parmesan or romano cheese
Freshly grated black pepper
        *Generally available in Italian delis

1. Make crust: dissolve yeast in water. Combine flour and water in food processor until blended. Add yeast mix and egg, mix until dough ball forms.
2. Knead lightly on floured board until smooth. Roll out to a suitable crust for pie plates. Can top completely or create lattice.
3. Mix ricotta, mozzarella, prosciutto, fresh cheese, eggs, grated cheese, and pepper thoroughly, to taste.
4. No mixers. No food processors. Use only hands to mix.
5. Pour into pie crust and cover with crust topper.
6. Let set for 60 minutes.
7. Brush top with egg wash.
8. Bake at 350° F for 45 minutes, or until pie crust is browned.

Notes:

_____

_____

_____

_____

_____

_____

Escarole with Beans

Camille Watson

2 pounds escarole, cleaned & chopped
1 cup pancetta, diced
2 cups cannellini beans
4 garlic cloves, crushed
4 cups chicken broth
Extra virgin olive oil
Salt and pepper
Pecorino cheese, grated

1. Soak escarole in chicken broth overnight to soften.
2. In a large pan, sauté pancetta with 1 tablespoon of olive oil.
3. Cook 2 minutes.
4. Add crushed garlic and sauté for 2 minutes more.
5. Add escarole and continue to sauté for a few minutes, until soft and reduces in size.
6. Add chicken broth and cannellini beans. Cook on medium heat for 15 minutes.
7. Salt and pepper to taste.
8. Serve with grated cheese.

Notes:

Fried Blossoms

1¼ cups all-purpose flour
1 teaspoon salt
12-ounce chilled pilsner, lager-style beer, or club soda
Blossoms* eggplant or zucchini, stamens removed, 2 dozen is sufficient.
Sea salt
Vegetable oil, for frying

1. In a large frying pot, heat about 2-inches of oil over medium heat until hot. A deep-fry thermometer reading of 350° F is adequate.
2. Combine flour and salt in a medium bowl, then whisk in beer or soda until almost smooth; small lumps are welcome. Don't over whisk or risk deflating the batter.
3. One by one, dredge blossoms in batter, lightly shaking off the excess.
4. Gently lay them in the oil, without crowding the pan.
5. Cook until golden brown, , flipping once with a slotted spoon, about 2 to 3 minutes.
6. Transfer to paper towels to drain. Sprinkle with sea salt and eat while hot.

For a Lighter Crispier Crust:
Fold 3 stiffly beaten egg whites into batter and proceed as above.

For Stuffed Blossoms:
To fill about 16 blossoms: combine 1 cup ricotta, 1 tablespoon freshly chopped mint, and ½ teaspoon finely grated lemon zest in a bowl. Season with salt and freshly ground black pepper. Using a spoon, fill each blossom with about 1 tablespoon ricotta mixture. Dip in batter and fry as instructed above.

In Italy, fried blossoms are the jalapeño poppers of the jet set - they are crunchy, salty, and utterly addictive. This is a modern take on Eleonora's recipe.

Notes:
_____
_____
_____
_____
_____
_____
_____

Gravies & Sauces

Brian Watson and Martha Nuzzo DiBiccari

Tomato Gravy (Sauce):
5 28-ounce cans of tomatoes
3 onions, roughly chopped
2 heads of garlic
1 cup red wine
Basil
Oregano
Salt
Pepper
Olive oil
Sugar (if necessary)

1. Sauté onions and garlic in oil until soft.
2. Add wine and reduce in half.
3. Add seasonings.
4. Add tomatoes.
5. Use stick blender to incorporate all ingredients.
6. Add sugar, if taste is acidic.

Marinara Sauce
1. Marinara is made with sautéed garlic with a dash of red pepper flakes.
2. Add crushed tomatoes, either whole tomatoes crushed by hand, or canned.
3. Simmer with salt and pepper for 20 to 30 minutes.
4. Serve.

Gravy:
1. All of marinara ingredients.
2. Add ½ cup red wine and let simmer for 1 hour.
3. Add meatballs, sausage, and/ or braciole and simmer on low for 3 hours.

Notes:

_____
_____
_____
_____
_____
_____
_____
_____
_____
_____
_____
_____
_____
_____
_____
_____
_____

Ham & Broccoli Casserole

2 10-ounce packages of frozen chopped broccoli
2 cups cut-up fully cooked smoked ham
1½ cups shredded cheddar cheese
1 cup baking mix
3 cups milk
4 eggs

1. Cook broccoli as directed on package, drain.
2. Spread in ungreased rectangular baking dish 13x9x2-inches.
3. Layer ham and cheese over broccoli.
4. Beat remaining ingredients with hand beater until smooth and slowly pour over cheese.
5. Bake uncovered at 350° F for 1 hour.

Serves 6 to 8

Ham & Broccolli Casserole

2 pkges (10 oz each) frozen chopped broccoli
2 cups cut-up fully cooked smoked ham
1½ cups shredded cheddar cheese
1 cup bisquick baking mix
3 cups milk
4 eggs.

1. preheat to 350°
2. Cook broccolli as directed on package; drain
3. Spread in ungreased rectangular baking dish, 13" x 9" x 2".
4. layer ham & cheese over broccolli
5. Beat remaining ingredients w/hand beater until smooth; slowly pour over cheese.
6. Bake uncovered 1 hr.

6 - 8 servings

Manicotti

<u>Crepe:</u>
5 cups water
3 cups all-purpose flour
6 eggs
¼ teaspoon salt (optional)

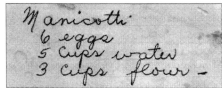

1. Mix together flour, water, eggs and salt to make a thin, smooth batter.
2. Pour about ¼ cup batter onto lightly greased griddle.
3. Cook until top forms film.

<u>Filling:</u>
2 eggs
2 pounds ricotta cheese
2 cups shredded mozzarella (approximately 10 ounces)
1 cup grated parmesan (about 2 ounces)
1 Tablespoon finely chopped fresh parsley
1 teaspoon grated nutmeg (optional)
1 cup grated pecorino romano cheese. More for serving, if preferred.

1. In a large bowl, combine filling ingredients.
2. Cover and refrigerate until ready to assemble the manicotti.
3. Heat oven to 375° F. Lightly brush two 9x13-inch baking dishes with oil.
4. Assemble the manicotti: Spread 3 to 4 tablespoons filling down the center of a crepe. Roll it up and place it, seam-side-down, in one of the baking dishes. Repeat with remaining crepes and filling.
5. Cover evenly with marinara sauce of choice.
6. Bake for 30 minutes. Sprinkle each baking dish with about ½ cup pecorino romano and continue baking until the sauce is bubbling and the cheese is just starting to brown, about 10 minutes more.

<u>Notes:</u>
_____
_____
_____
_____

Meatballs

1 teaspoon olive oil
1 large onion, finely chopped (about 1 cup)
½ pound of ground pork or bulk Italian pork sausage
2 garlic cloves, finely chopped
¼ cup chopped fresh parley
2 medium eggs
¾ cups of soft bread crumbs
2 teaspoons finely chopped fresh basil or 1 teaspoon dried basil (optional)
½ Tablespoon finely chopped fresh oregano or ½ teaspoon dried oregano
1 teaspoon salt
1 teaspoon pepper

1. Combine ingredients in a large bowl. Blend together with your hands until the meat has become thoroughly blended with all the seasonings. The mixture should be fairly moist.
2. To form the meatballs, wet hands in small bowl of lukewarm water. Then take a little more than ¼ cup of meatball mixture. Roll it in the palm of your hands to form a smooth ball about 2½ inches in diameter.
3. For a crusty meatball, fill frying pan with enough oil to cover ¼ of the meatball when frying. Oil must be hot when starting to fry and meatballs will crust very quickly. For a lighter option, fry in approximately 3 tablespoons of olive oil on medium heat for about 5 minutes, turning them regularly until evenly browned.
4. Drop meatballs into gently boiling tomato sauce 20 minutes to cook well.
5. Scrape bottom of the frying skillet and pour the crusty meat particles into the meat sauce.

Notes:

_____
_____
_____
_____
_____
_____
_____
_____
_____

Martha notes, "On Sunday mornings Dom, and Brian would meet Larry at mom's apartment for fresh meatballs and Italian bread. The time would be filled with teasing accompanied by the good food.

Eleonor's food was the foundation of all her love for her family.

Minute Steaks

Denise Ann Watson

1 2-pound package of cube steaks (beef)
1 cup bread crumbs
¼ cup grated parmesan cheese
1 teaspoon of dried oregano
2 eggs, beaten
½ cup of cooking oil
Salt and pepper to taste
3 to 4 cups of brown gravy

1. Beat eggs in a flat bottom pan or bowl for easy coating.
2. In another flat bottom bowl or pan, mix together bread crumbs, parmesan cheese, oregano, salt, and pepper. Set aside.
3. Remove cube steaks from packaging.
4. Pound steaks with the raised side of a meat tenderizer hammer.
5. Heat oil in large skillet over medium-high heat.
6. Coat cube stakes with eggs and then with the dried ingredients.
7. Fry steaks until browned on each side.
8. Layer steaks in coated baking dish.
9. Coat completely with brown gravy.
10. Bake at 350° F for 15 to 20 minutes. Check at regular intervals.
11. Remove from oven when gravy begins to bubble.

Notes:

_____

_____

_____

_____

_____

_____

_____

_____

Pasta e Ceci
Dominick Watson

1 cup dried chickpeas, soaked in water overnight and drained
1 fresh bay leaf
1 garlic clove
1 sprig rosemary
¼ teaspoon red pepper flakes
2 Tablespoons extra virgin olive oil, and additional for drizzling
½ medium yellow onion, finely diced (optional)
1 cup tomatoes, about 4, crushed by hand
Salt and black pepper to taste
7 ounces pasta, the size of small elbows
Grated parmesan, for garnish

As he recounted this recipe, Dominick proclaimed, "This was my most hated meal as a child. And, it still is."

1. Place the soaked chickpeas in a saucepan and cover with water by 1 inch. Add seasonings, bring to a simmer and covered. If dry, add ½ cup water. Simmer until the chickpeas are soft and creamy, 1½ to 2 hours. Season with salt. Remove and discard the bay leaf and rosemary.
2. In another pan, heat olive oil over medium heat. Once hot, add onions and cook until translucent, about 10 minutes. Add tomatoes, season with salt and cook, stirring occasionally, until the tomatoes have thickened slightly, about 8 minutes.
3. Add a ladle full of the chickpea mixture with garlic clove and puree with blender until smooth. Add chickpea puree and tomatoes back into the saucepan with the rest of the chickpeas and bring to a simmer.
4. Add the pasta and cook, stirring frequently to keep from sticking, until the pasta is al dente and the sauce has thickened, 12 to 15 minutes, depending on pasta.
5. Season with salt and pepper. The dish should be creamy and more soup-like than typical pasta with sauce.
6. To serve, garnish with parmesan and a drizzle of olive oil.

Notes:

Pasta Fagioli

Camille Watson

16 ounces cannellini beans
2 cups pancetta, small cubes
6 celery stalks
1 onion, large
4 peeled tomatoes
16 ounces pasta. Ditalini, elbows, or small shells are best.
1 cup water
Extra virgin olive oil
Salt and pepper
Grated parmesan cheese

1. Sauté pancetta in olive oil.
2. Finely chop vegetables, then add to frying pan.
3. Sauté with pancetta for a few minutes, then add half the beans.
4. Mash other half of the beans, then add to pan with cup of hot water.
5. Let simmer 20 minutes.
6. Boil pasta "al dente." Add to bean mixture and simmer 2 minutes.
7. Salt and pepper to taste.
8. Serve with grated parmesan cheese

Note: If a thinner soup is desired, add more hot water ¼ cup at a time.

Notes:

Pastina with Broth

Camille Watson

3 quarts water
¾ pounds of alphabet pastina
¼ cup onion, finely chopped
½ cup tomatoes, finely chopped
½ cup carrots, finely chopped
2 Tablespoons parsley, finely chopped
2 bay leaves
2 Tablespoons extra virgin olive oil

1. Add all ingredients except pasta to large pot.
2. Bring mixture to a boil. Continue to cook for 15 minutes.
3. Add pastina, let cook until al dente.
4. Serve with grated parmesan cheese.

Notes:

_____

_____

_____

_____

_____

_____

_____

Pizza Fritte

Brian Watson

6 cups flour
4 envelopes active dry yeast
5 tablespoons sugar
4 tablespoons salt
6 tablespoons olive oil
2¾ cups water at 100° F to 110° F

1. Add yeast and warm water in a bowl, allow to bloom for at least 15 minutes.
2. Mix salt, flour, oil, and water-yeast mixture to large bowl and mix.
3. Knead on a floured surface until smooth and elastic, approximately 6 to 8 minutes.
4. Add additional flour as needed.
5. Put in an oiled bowl. Cover with plastic wrap and towels and let rise for at least 90 minutes.
6. Segment dough into pieces that roll into thin 5-inch rounds, about ⅜-inch thick.
7. Heat about ⅜-inch of vegetable oil to 375°F in a pan on stove or in an electric frying pan.
8. Pick 1 dough disk and carefully lower it into oil. Let cook for 60 seconds. Once it puffs up on top and becomes light brown on the bottom. Flip it over and cook until light brown on the other side, about 60 seconds.
9. Remove and place on paper towel.
10. Serve warm, with topping of choice such as maple syrup, confectioners' sugar, cinnamon sugar; or with marinara sauce, tomato gravy and cheeses.

Notes:

_____

_____

_____

_____

_____

_____

_____

Pot Cheese Balls

1 cup of pot cheese
2 eggs
2 teaspoons sugar
1 cup flour
1 Tablespoons salt
2 Tablespoons baking powder
Small bowl of flour or bread crumbs for coating
Cooking oil

1. Combine all the ingredients.
2. Shape into balls.
3. Coat with flour or bread crumbs.
4. In a large skillet, heat about 2-inches of oil until hot.
5. Lower pot cheese balls into hot oil. Keep separate while cooking.
6. Fry until golden.
7. Remove with slotted spoon to a paper towel covered plate.
8. Allow to cool. Serve while warm.

Notes:

_____
_____
_____
_____
_____
_____
_____
_____
_____
_____
_____
_____
_____

Pot cheese balls

1 cup of pot cheese
2 eggs
2 tea spoon sugar
1 cup of flour
1 tb salt
2 '' baking powder
let oil get hot and fry
until golden

Soup with Orzo Pasta

Camille Watson

8 ounces sweet sausage
1 cup pecorino, grated
½ cup bread crumbs, plain
4 garlic cloves, chopped fine
4 large eggs
2 quart chicken stock
2 Tablespoons extra virgin olive oil
1 medium onion, chopped
2 medium potatoes, cubed
1 cup carrots, chopped
1 cup celery, chopped
2 cups spinach
½ pound orzo pasta

1. Combine first 5 ingredients, roll small meatballs, then set aside.
2. In a large pot, add oil and sauté onion on medium 5 minutes, until soft.
3. Add stock and potatoes, bring to a boil.
4. Add carrots, celery and meatballs, then bring to a boil.
5. Add spinach and pasta.
6. Cook until pasta is al dente.

Notes:

_____

_____

_____

_____

_____

_____

Spinach Squares

2 10-ounce packages frozen chopped spinach
10 eggs, whipped
8 ounces shredded mozzarella cheese
1 stick pepperoni cut into small pieces
½ cup Italian bread crumbs
½ cup grated Italian cheese
Pepper to taste

1. Cook spinach. Drain and set aside.
2. Mix eggs, bread crumbs, and cheese together.
3. Add spinach and pepperoni. Combine.
4. Pour mixture into greased 9x13-inch pan.
5. Bake at 350° F for 40 minutes.

Notes:

_____
_____
_____
_____
_____
_____
_____
_____

Vegetable Quiche

1 pastry layer for a 9-inch pie
1 cup cooked rice
1 4-ounce can of mushrooms
1 medium onion chopped
1 box frozen chopped broccoli, cooked and drained
2 beaten eggs
¾ cup milk
1 cup shredded cheddar cheese
Salt and pepper to taste

1. Sauté mushrooms and onions.
2. In large bowl, beat eggs, and milk.
3. Add cheese, cooked rice, cooked broccoli, salt, and pepper.
4. Combine evenly.
5. Pour mixture into unbaked pastry-lined pie pan.
6. Bake at 350° F for 35 to 40 minutes.

Serves 4 to 6.

Vegetable Quiche

1 pastry layer for 9" pie
1 cup cooked rice
1 4-ounce can mushrooms
1 med. chopped onion
1 box frozen chopped brocolli,
    cooked as directed

2 beaten eggs
¾ cup milk
1 cup shredded
    cheddar cheese
salt & pepper to taste

1. sautee mushrooms & onions
2. in large bowl, beat eggs & milk
3. add cheese, cooked rice, cooked brocolli & salt & pepper
4. pour mixture into unbaked pastry
5. Bake at 350° 35-40 min.

Serves 4-6

Notes:

_____

_____

_____

_____

Zucchini Quiche

3 cups diced zucchini
1 cup onions, chopped
1 cup baking mix
4 eggs
½ cup oil
½ cup grated cheese
Pepper

1. Mix the baking mix as directed. Roll out for crust.
2. Place dough in 9-inch greased pie plate.
3. Combine remaining ingredients.
4. Pour into pie plate.
5. Bake at 350° F for 30 minutes.

chick
3 cups slice Zuccini
1 onion Chopped
1 cup Bisque mix
4 eggs
½ cup oil
½ cup grated cheese
pepper

Cook 30mins in pie
plate 350° 30mins

Notes:

The Incredible Cookies

Anisette Chocolate Brownie Cookies

Martha Nuzzo DiBiccari

4 cups flour
4 eggs
1 cup granulated sugar
1 cup brown sugar
2 sticks butter or margarine
2 teaspoons baking powder
1 12-ounce package of chocolate chips
1 ounce anisette or anise extract

1. Cream butter.
2. Beat in sugars.
3. Add eggs and anisette, and beat in.
4. Add flour and baking powder.
5. Stir in chocolate chips.
6. Shape or roll into small loaves, about 5.
7. If dough is sticky, add a little flour or flour hands as needed.
8. Bake on greased cookie sheets at 350° F for 30 minutes.
9. Slice when cooled.

Notes:

Anisette Cookies

8 cups flour
1 dozen eggs
13 teaspoons baking powder
2 cups sugar
1 pound butter or ½ cup margarine
Anisette to taste, about 1 teaspoon
Confectioners' sugar and water for icing

1. Mix first five ingredients in large bowl until dough is sticky.
2. Pinch into 1-inch pieces. Shape into round cookies.
3. Place about 1-inch apart on ungreased cookie sheet. Flatten slightly.
4. Bake at 375° F on ungreased cookie sheet.

Icing:
1. Blend 1 teaspoon anise extract with enough hot water to 1 cup confectioners' sugar to form a smooth icing.
2. Cover cookies while warm, not hot.

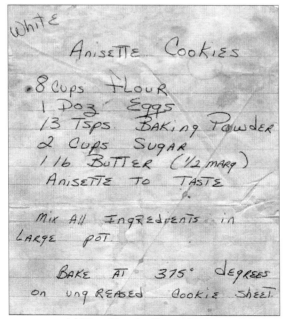

*Additional handwritten recipes are
on the following page.*

Anisette Cookies (By Carrie O. Tell.)

6 Eggs
1 cup Oil
Anisette
1 Cup Sugar
3-4 Cups Flour
3 Tsp. Baking Powder
1 Cup nuts, chopped

Mix Eggs, Oil, Anise. Add
Other Ingredients.
Bake 350° —

Anisette Cookies

1 cup sugar
4 eggs
1½ cups flour
¾ cup oil

2 teaspoon baking powder
- teaspoon anisette
grease pan
    bake 350
tin foil pan fill half way
        Pan size   5X10 1 inch deep -

Cookies White anisette

8 cups flour
1 doz eggs
13 tsps baking Powder
2 cups sugar
1 lb butter
anisette to taste

Notes:

_____
_____
_____
_____
_____
_____
_____
_____
_____

Anisette Toast

Martha Nuzzo DiBiccari

2 ½ cups all-purpose flour
2 teaspoon baking powder
¼ teaspoon salt
1 cup sugar
¼ cup butter or margarine
3 medium-size eggs
1 teaspoon anise extract or anisette

1. Sift flour, baking powder, and salt 3 times.
2. Cream butter and sugar, and eggs one at a time.
3. Add anise extract.
4. Add flour mixture a little at a time, mixing well. Dough will be a little sticky.
5. Divide dough in half.
6. Shape into two loaves and place on greased cookie sheets.
7. Bake at 350° F for 15 to 20 minutes.
8. Cut into 1-inch slices, turn on side.
9. Bake again for 10 to 15 minutes until golden brown.
10. Cool on wire rack.

Notes:

Anna Angotta Cookies
The favorite version of Eleonora's anisette cookies

2 sticks of butter
1 cup sugar
6 eggs
½ pint heavy cream
1 shot anisette
6 teaspoons baking powder
6 cups flour

<u>Icing:</u>
Confectioners' sugar and water

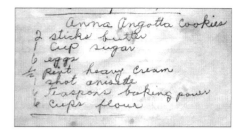

1. Mix all ingredients, except for icing, in large bowl until dough is sticky.
2. Pinch into 1-inch pieces. Shape into round cookies.
3. Place about 1-inch apart on ungreased cookie sheet. Flatten slightly.
4. Bake at 375° F on ungreased cookie sheet.

Icing:
1. Blend 1 teaspoon anise extract with enough hot water to 1 cup confectioners' sugar to form a smooth icing.
2. Cover cookies while warm, not hot.

<u>Notes:</u>

_____
_____
_____
_____
_____
_____
_____
_____
_____

Biscotti

6 uova (eggs)
1 tazza di zucchero (cup of sugar)
1 tazza di "Crisco" olio (cup of shortening)
6 tucchiaini di lievito in polvere (teaspoon of baking powder)*
Li limone grattugiato e spremuto farina a quando ne prende (Grate lemon and squeeze into flour as soon as it takes it)
Forno 400 gr. per 20 to 25 minuti (Oven 400° F for 20 to 25 minutes)

1. In a medium-sized bowl, beat the butter, sugar, and salt.
2. Add baking powder until the mixture is smooth and creamy.
3. Beat in the eggs.
4. Add flour and then grated lemon, stir until a smooth, sticky dough forms.
5. Place dough onto a large, lightly greased, baking sheet.
6. Divide dough in half and shape it into 2 9½x2-inch logs, about ¾-inch tall. Straighten logs, smooth tops and sides; a wet spatula works nicely.
7. Sprinkle with coarse white sugar, if desired, pressing into surface gently.
8. Bake the dough at 400° F for 25 minutes. Remove from the oven.
9. Using a spray bottle filled with room-temperature water, lightly spritz loaves covering the sides as well as the top. Softening the crust slightly makes slicing the biscotti easier.
10. Reduce the oven temperature to 325° F.
11. Wait 5 minutes, then use a sharp chef or serrated knife to cut the log crosswise into ½- to ¾-inch slices. Be creative, cut on the diagonal for fewer, longer biscotti, if you choose.
12. Be certain to cut evenly.
13. Set the biscotti on edge on the prepared baking sheet.
14. Return to the oven and bake them for 25 to 30 minutes, until they feel dry with a slightly moist center; and begins to turn golden.
15. Remove biscotti from the oven and transfer to a rack to cool.
16. Store airtight at room temperature.

```
Biscotti
  6 Uova
  1 Tazza di Zucchero
  1 Tazza di Crisco Olio
  6 Cucchiaini di bacon paud
  li limone grattugiato e spremuto farina a
  quando ne prende.

  Forno 400 gr. per 20, 25 minuti.
```

A family translator indicated that the notation "bacon paud" is actually baking powder.

Butter Balls

1 cup butter
4 tablespoon powdered sugar
2 cups sifted flour
1 teaspoon vanilla
1 cup chopped nuts

1.	Cream butter, add sugar, and continue to blend until light.
2.	Add vanilla and sifted flour. Mix well.
3.	Fold in nuts.
4.	Shape into balls.
5.	Cook on ungreased cookie sheet at 350° F for 15 to 18 minutes.
6.	When cooled, dust with powdered sugar.

Butter Cookies

1 pound of sweet butter
1 yolk of an egg
1 small glass of whiskey
1 small dish of almonds, chopped
1 small dish of confectioners' sugar
"Then" flour, most likely 2 cups
Lots of confectioners' sugar for coating

1. Brown the almonds in the little pan, let cool, then chop very small.
2. Mix the butter for 1 hour with mixer. Then add yolk, then sugar, then whiskey, then almonds, and then the flour.
3. Stop the mixer and mix dough by hand.
4. Note: the softer the dough, the better the cookies.
5. Design the cookies. Bake at 350° F until golden brown.
6. Lay cookies on wax paper to cool some.
7. Sprinkle confectioners' sugar on top. A lot of sugar!

Notes:

Christmas Wreaths

Joyce Nuzzo Taborsak

2 cups flour
½ teaspoon baking powder
1 cup butter
½ cup sugar
2 tablespoons water
1 teaspoon vanilla
1 egg
1½ cup finely chopped nuts
Jam or jelly

(Christmas Wreaths)
Recipe for Bright-Eyed Susans   Makes 48 cookies
From: Joyce
2 c. flour   ½ c. sugar   1 egg
½ tsp baking powder   2 tbsp. water   1½ c. finely
1 c. butter   1 tsp. vanilla chopped nuts
       jam or jelly
preheat oven to 350°F. Sift flour & baking powder
twice. Cream butter & sugar until light & fluffy.
Add water, vanilla, & egg yolk. Add flour & mix.
form the dough into balls @ size of a walnut. →

Roll in the beaten egg white and then into nuts.
Place on lightly greased baking sheets and
bake for 5 minutes. Remove from oven and
press thumbprint in each ball. Return to the
oven and bake a further 8-10 minutes.
Remove to cooling trays and fill the center
with bright jam or jelly.

1. Preheat oven to 350° F.
2. Sift flour and baking powder twice.
3. Cream butter and sugar until light and fluffy.
4. Add water, vanilla, and egg yolk. Add flour and mix.
5. Form dough into balls about the size of a walnut.
6. Beat egg white.
7. Roll dough balls into egg white and then into nuts.
8. Place on lightly greased baking sheets.
9. Bake for 5 minutes.
10. Remove from oven and press thumb print into each.
11. Return to oven and bake further, 8 to 10 minutes.
12. Remove to cooling trays and fill the center with bright jam or jelly.

Notes:

X-MAS WREATHS
CREAM
1 c. BUTTER
½ c. BROWN SUGAR
2 eggs separated (use
       yolks & save whites)

Add
2 c. flour
½ tsp. SALT
2 c. chopped walnuts

Roll into small balls drop
into egg whites, then roll in
nuts. Place on cookie sheets
cook for 5 mins. Than make
small holes on top of cookie.
fill with jelly finish
cooking. (5 mins)

Cornflake Macaroons

½ cup margarine
1 cup brown sugar
1 cup white sugar
2 eggs
1 cup pecans
1 cup coconut
2 quarts cornflakes

1. Mix ingredients together well.
2. Drop by teaspoon onto cookie sheets line with wax paper or a heavily buttered baking sheet.
3. Bake 6 or 8 only at 350° F for 10 minutes.
4. Let cool slightly and carefully remove.
5. If you can't remove the cookies before they harden, put back in the over for a couple of minutes.

Notes:

Date Bars

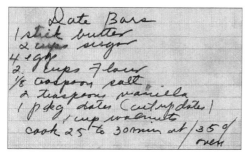

1 stick butter
2 cups sugar
4 eggs
2 cups flour
⅛ teaspoon salt
2 teaspoon vanilla
1 package of dates, cut up
1 cup walnuts

1. Mix together dates, sugar, eggs, and vanilla.
2. Sift flour and salt together in a large bowl. Cut in butter until crumbly. Sprinkle water over mixture; stir lightly.
3. Combine together.
4. Add walnuts if desired.
5. Pat into a greased 13x9-inch baking pan.
6. Cook at 350° F for 25 to 30 minutes until lightly browned.
7. Cool on a wire rack. Cut into bars.

Notes:

Molasses Butter Balls

1 cup butter
½ teaspoon vanilla extract
¼ cup molasses
2 cups sifted all-purpose flour
½ teaspoon salt
2 cups pecans, finely chopped

1. Cream butter with extract, add molasses, and beat well.
2. Blend flour and salt, add in fourths to creamed mixture, mixing until blended after each addition.
3. Stir in pecans.
4. Shape dough into 1-inch balls.
5. Place on lightly greased cookie sheets.
6. Bake at 350° F for 12 to 15 minutes.
7. Cool slightly, roll in confectioners' sugar.

Notes:

_____

_____

_____

_____

_____

Peanut Butter Balls

Martha Nuzzo DiBiccari

½ stick of soft butter
1 pound of confectioners' sugar
2 cups chunky peanut butter, about 1 pound 2 ounces
3 cups of crispie rice cereal
Chocolate chips for coating

1. Mix all ingredients together, except chocolate.
2. Shape into small ball-shaped cookies.
3. Place on wax paper-lined cookie sheet and refrigerate for 60 minutes.
4. Melt chocolate chips.
5. Dip cookie with fork into chocolate.
6. Store in refrigerator or freezer.

Notes:

_____

_____

_____

_____

_____

_____

_____

_____

_____

_____

_____

_____

_____

_____

Pignoli

½ cup confectioners' sugar
½ cup granulated sugar
¼ cup un-sifted all-purpose flour
⅛ teaspoon salt
1 8-ounce can almond paste
2 egg whites
1 3-ounce jar Italian pignoli nuts

*The handwritten recipe is
on the following page.*

1. Preheat oven to 300° F.
2. Grease 2 large cookie sheets.
3. Sift granulated sugar and ½ cup confectioners' sugar with flour and salt. Set aside.
4. In a medium bowl, break up almond paste into small pieces with a fork.
5. Add egg whites and beat with electric mixer at medium speed until well blended and smooth.
6. With wooden spoon, stir in flour mixture until well blended.
7. Using slightly rounded teaspoon to section dough, roll portions into balls between hands making approximately 1-inch in diameter.
8. Place 2-inches apart on cookie sheet.
9. Press cookies into rounds 1½ inches in diameter.
10. Press nuts into tops.
11. Bake 20 to 25 minutes or until golden.
12. Remove to wire rack to cool.
13. Sprinkle with confectioners' sugar.
14. Store in tightly covered container to mellow in freeze so they remain soft when defrosting.

Makes 2½ dozen

Notes:

_____
_____
_____
_____
_____
_____
_____

Pine Pignoli (Pine nut cookies)

Cookie dough

½ cup of confectioners sugar
½ cup of granulated sugar
¼ cup of unsifted all purpose flour
⅛ teas of salt
1 can 8oz almond paste.
2 egg whites
1 jar 3oz Italian pignoli nuts

① Preheat oven to 300°F
Grease 2 large cookie sheets
② make dough, Sift granulated sugar
And ½ cup of confectioners sugar with
flour + salt (set aside)
③ using fork break up almond paste
into small pieces, in med bowl add
egg whites + beat with electric mixer
at medium speed until well blended +
smooth, with wooden spoon stir in flour
mixture, until well blended. using
slightly rounded teaspoonful, roll dough
between hands into balls, about 1 inch in
diameter, Place 2 inches apart on cool sheet
lightly press into 1½ inches in diameter, press
nuts on top + press   a little Bake 20 to 25 min oven

or until golden. remove to wire rack to
cool, Sprinkle with confectioners sugar
store in a tightly covered container to mellow
in freeze so they remain soft when defrosting
makes 2½ dozen

enjoy!!

Ricotta Cheese Cookies

Ricotta Cheese Cookies

1/2 LB margarine   2 cups sugar
2 eggs   1 teas baking soda
1 LB Ricotta cheese   1 teas salt
2 Teas. Vanilla   4 cups flour
           (see note)

Icing:
1/2 cup Confectioner's Sugar
1/4 teasp. Vanilla
2-3 Teaspoons milk
Sprinkles Optional

1. Mix wet Dough Ingredients & Add To Dry Ingredients. Mix well.
2. By using A Hefty Teaspoonful, Form Round Balls. Place on Greased Cookie Sheet. Bake at 350-Degree oven for 12-15 min.
3. Combine Ingredients For Icing. Dip Hot Cookies into Icing. Top with Sprinkles if Desired. Makes About 100 cookies

Note: Add More Flour, Depending on How stiff you Like Dough in order To Form Balls.

½ pound margarine
2 eggs
1 pound ricotta cheese
2 teaspoon vanilla
2 cups sugar
1 teaspoon baking soda
1 teaspoon salt
4 cups flour*

Icing:
½ cup confectioners' sugar
¼ teaspoon vanilla
2 to 3 teaspoon milk
Sprinkles optional
    (sprinkles required for Eleonora cookies)

1. Mix wet dough ingredients.
2. Add wet ingredients to dry ingredients and mix well. *Add more flour depending on how stiff you prefer the dough for forming balls.
3. Using a hefty teaspoon full of dough, form balls.
4. Place on greased cookie sheet.
5. Bake at 350° F in oven for 12 to 15 minutes.
6. Combine ingredients for icing.
7. Dip hot cookies into icing. Top with sprinkles if desired.

Notes:

_____
_____
_____
_____
_____
_____
_____
_____

Sesame Cookies

6 cups flour
2 cup sugar
1 Tablespoon Vanilla
6 teaspoon baking powder
6 eggs
1 cup shortening
Milk and sesame seeds for coating

1. Mix salt, flour, and baking powder.
2. Cut in shortening, then add sugar.
3. Roll small ropes, about 2 inches long.
4. Wet your hand a little.
5. Put in milk, then roll in seeds.
6. Bake on sheet pan ½-inch apart in
    oven at 350° F for 25 minutes.

Notes:

Seven Layer Cookies

9 x 13 pan
Melt 1 stick of margarine in pan

Layer in:
1. 1 cup graham cracker crumbs.
2. 1 cup coconut.
3. 1 cup butterscotch morsels.
4. 1 cup chocolate chip morsels.
5. Drizzle 14-ounce can sweetened condensed milk over everything.
6. Top with 1½ cups of chopped nuts.
7. Bake at 350° F for 25 to 30 minutes.
8. Let cool.
9. Cut while hot.

7 Layer Cookies
9 x 13 pan
Melt one stick margarine
in pan. then layers sprinkle
1 cup graham crumbs
1 cup coconut
1 cup butterscotch morsels
1 cup choc. chip morsels
drizzle 14 oz. sweet
condensed milk over this +
then 1½ cups chop nuts.
Bake 350°, 25 - 30 min.
Cool + cut.
CuT wHiLe HoT

Notes:

_____
_____
_____
_____
_____
_____
_____
_____
_____
_____

Sour Cream Cookies

1 1/3 cups shortening
2 2/3 cups sugar
4 eggs
6 2/3 cups flour
4 teaspoon baking powder
1 teaspoon baking soda
2 teaspoon salt
2 teaspoon nutmeg
2 cups sour cream
2 cups finely chopped nuts (optional)

Topping
4 tablespoon sugar
1 teaspoon nutmeg

1. Dissolve baking soda and salt in sour cream.
2. Mix shortening and sugar. Blend in eggs.
3. Mix in sour cream mixture.
4. Slowly add flour and salt, mix well.
5. Chill for at least one hour.
6. Roll out and cut with your favorite shapes. Be sure not to roll too thin.
7. Sprinkle with nutmeg and sugar.
8. Top with nuts (optional).
9. Bake at 350° F for 10 minutes.

Notes:

_____
_____
_____
_____
_____
_____
_____
_____

Struffoli

Pat Moccia

From the kitchen of... Pat Moccia

STRuffoLi

3 Eggs
1/2 Stick BuTTER
3 Tsp. BAKing PowdeR
3 cups FlouR
3/4 cup SugAR
KNEAD - RoLL inTo 3/4 inch STicks, CuT
inTo 1/4 inch BALLs, FRy in DEEP OiL
DRAin in ColAndER, PouR
DARK KARo SyRuP
(oveR)

3 eggs
½ stick butter
3 teaspoon baking powder
3 cups flour
¾ cup sugar
Karo syrup

1. Combine ingredients and knead.
2. Roll into ¾-inch sticks.
3. Cut into ¼-inch balls.
4. Fry in deep oil.
5. Drain in colander.
6. Pour dark Karo syrup into frying pan.
7. Warm syrup and roll balls in syrup.

InTo Frying PAn. WARm SyRuP + RoLL BALLS in SyRuP.

Notes:

Tea Dainties

1 stick of butter
1 cup regular flour
1 3-ounce package cream cheese

1. Mix well together.
2. Form little round balls or roll like a pie crust and cut with a glass.
3. Fit into small cup cake pan, ungreased

Filling:
3/4 cup light brown sugar
1 Tablespoon soft butter
1 teaspoon vanilla
Dash of salt
1 egg
2/3 cup chopped nuts

1. Mix all ingredients together and half-fill the dough in cup cake pan.
2. Bake 325° F for 25 minutes.

Notes:
_____
_____
_____
_____
_____
_____
_____

Tea Dainties

Dough:
  1 stick of Butter
  1 cup of flour regular
  1 3/oz pack of cream cheese

Mix well together.
form round Balls or
roll like a pie crust.
and cut with a glass.
and fit into small cup
Cake pan (ungreased)

Filling:
  3/4 cup of light brown sugar
  1 tablespoon of soft butter
  1 teaspoon of vanilla
  1 dash of salt
  1 egg

2/3 cup of chopped nuts.
Mix together. and fill
into dough. which is
a cup cake pan + half full.
Bake into oven. at
325° for 25 minutes.

TEA DAINTIES

DOUGH   1 stick butter
        1 cup reg. flour
        3 oz. pkg. cream cheese

  Mix well together - form little round balls and press into small
  cupcake pan.

FILLING   3/4 cup light brown sugar
          1 tbsp. soft butter
          1 tsp vanilla
          dash salt
          2/3 cup chopped nuts
          1 egg

Mix together and fill pan (about half full - each little pan)

Bake at 325 degrees for about 25 minutes

TEA DAINTIES

Dough: 1 stick butter
         1 cup reg. flour
         3 oz. pkg. cream cheese

  Mix well together - Form little round balls and press into small
  cupcake pan.

Filling: 3/4 cup light brown sugar
         1 tbsp. soft butter
         1 tsp. vanilla
         Dash salt
         2/3 cup chopped nuts
         1 egg

    Mix together and fill pan (about half full - each little pan)

    Bake at 325 degrees for about 25 minutes.

Eleonora's Amazing Eats

51

Tiny Tea Tasties

Cups:
3 ounces cream cheese
1/2 cup butter
1 cup flour

1.   Mix together and create 2 ounce balls.
2.   Shape into the cups of a small cupcake pan.

Filling:
3/4 cup of light brown sugar
1 teaspoon vanilla
1 tablespoon softened butter
1 egg
2/3 ounces chopped nuts

1.   Fill cups half-way with filling.
2.   Bake at 350° F for 25 minutes.

Turdilli

Turdilli di Elira:
1 tazzio aiolio (cup of extra virgin olive oil and garlic sauce)
1 tazzio vino (cup of wine)
1 cup shortening
1 cup aqua (water)
1 Tablespoon sugar
1 orango grattugiato (grated orange)
1 pinch baking soda
1 pinch salt
Farina quando amt va
    (Flour in the amount it takes)
Oil for frying

Turdilli di Elis Ilia:
1 cup oil
2 cups muscato (white sweet wine)
1 pinch of cinnamon
1 orange grattugiato (grated)
Flour (in the amount it takes)
Oil for frying

1. Combine ingredients.
2. Work dough gently to form dough.
3. Roll into small balls.
4. Fry in oil until golden brown.
5. Remove from oil and drain.
6. Optional: in frying pan, warm
    honey or syrup and coat fried balls.

Notes:

_____
_____
_____
_____
_____

Vermouth Mix: A Drunk Cookie

1 glass vermouth
1 glass white wine
1 glass shortening
½ glass oil
1 Tablespoon sugar
1 teaspoon cinnamon
2 egg yolks
1 grated orange
1 teaspoon baking power

This recipe is a mystery to the Moccia- Watson family. It may have been an addition to a cookie recipe. May you enjoy exploring the options.

Notes:

_____

_____

_____

_____

_____

_____

_____

_____

_____

_____

_____

Walnut Twist Cookies

Walnut Twist Cookies

2 cups flour
½ lb margarine
½ pint sour cream
1 egg yolk or whole egg

¾ cup sugar
1 tsp cinnamon
1 cup ground walnuts

1. Cut marg. into flour, work well w/sour cream & mix into flour mixture
2. Separate dough into 4 balls, chill.
3. take 1 ball out at a time, roll out in a circle. Sprinkle w/mixture of sugar, cinnamon, & walnuts, roll from widest end to center.
4. Put on ungreased cookie sheet & bake 25 min at 350°. Sprinkle with confectioners sugar.

2 cups flour
½ pound margarine
½ pint sour cream
1 egg yolk or whole egg
¾ cup sugar
1 teaspoon cinnamon
1 cup ground walnuts
Confectioners' sugar to coat

1. Cut margarine into flour.
2. Work eggs well with sour cream and mix into flour mixture.
3. Separate dough into 5 balls and chill.
4. Take 1 ball out at a time. Roll out into a circle.
5. Sprinkle with mixture of sugar, cinnamon and walnuts.
6. Roll from widest end to center.
7. Put on ungreased cookie sheet and bake 25 minutes at 350° F.
8. Sprinkle with confectioners' sugar.

Notes:

The Desserts & Treats

Apple Betty

4 cups sliced pared tart apples
½ cup orange juice
1 cup sugar
1½ cup all-purpose flour
½ teaspoon cinnamon
½ teaspoon nutmeg
½ cup butter
Dash of salt

1. Mound apples in a buttered 9-inch pie plate.
2. Sprinkle with orange juice.
3. Combine sugar, flour, and spices, along with a dash of salt.
4. Cut in butter until mixture is crumbly and sprinkle over apples.
5. Bake at 375° F for 45 minutes or until apples are tender and topping is crisp-tender.

Notes:

Apple Cake

Fresh apple Cake

½ cup shortening
1 cup sugar
½ cup firmly packed brown sugar
2 teaspoon baking soda
1 teaspoon baking powder
1 cup buttermilk
2 eggs beaten
2¼ cups flour
½ teaspoon nutmeg
½ teaspoon cinnamon
¼ teaspoon cloves
¼ teaspoon salt
2 to 3 cups apples chopped

Topping:
½ cup nuts
½ cup sugar
¼ cups firmly packed brown sugar
⅛ teaspoon cinnamon

1. Preheat oven to 350° F.
2. Beat all ingredients except apples until mixed well.
3. Fold in apples.
4. Combine topping ingredients.
5. Pour batter into pan.
6. Sprinkle topping over batter.
7. Bake at 350° F for 25 to 45 minutes.

Notes:

Apple Muffins

2 cups cubed, peeled raw apples
2 eggs
2 cups brown sugar
½ cup oil
1½ teaspoon cinnamon
2 cups flour
1½ teaspoon baking soda
1 teaspoon salt

1. Mix all ingredients together.
2. Add a little water to thin the batter.
3. Fill muffin cups 2/3 the way.
4. Bake at 350° F for 25 minutes.

Makes 12 to 18 muffins

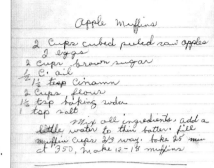

Notes:

_____
_____
_____
_____
_____
_____
_____
_____
_____
_____
_____
_____

Apple Pie

Crust:
2 teaspoons baking soda
1 teaspoon buttermilk
2 eggs beaten
2¼ cup flour
¼ teaspoon salt

Filling:
2 to 3 cups chopped apples
½ cup butter
1 cup sugar
½ cup brown sugar
½ teaspoon nutmeg
½ teaspoon cinnamon
¼ teaspoon cloves

Topping:
½ cup nuts, chopped
¼ cup sugar
1 teaspoon cinnamon
¼ cup brown sugar
Butter, at room temperature, as needed

1. Prepare the pie crust. Combine flour, baking soda, and salt. Add buttermilk and eggs until mixture resembles coarse crumbs. Add water a tablespoon at a time, until dough just comes together. Gather up, cover and chill for about 30 minutes.
2. Make the topping. Mix together nuts, sugar, and cinnamon. Blend in butter with fingertips until coarse crumbs form. Set aside.
3. Preheat the oven to 400° F. Roll out dough into a 12-inch circle on a lightly floured surface. Press into 9½-inch pie plate. Trim and fold under the edges. Chill while making the filling.
4. In a large bowl, whisk together sugars, cinnamon, nutmeg, cloves, and butter until combined. Add apple slices and toss until evenly coated. Spoon filling into pie shell, sprinkle evenly with crumb topping.
5. Bake pie on lower rack of oven 20 minutes.
6. Reduce temperature to 350° F and continue to bake 45 to 50 minutes or until apples are tender and topping is golden and crisp.
7. Cool on a wire rack.

Eleonora's Amazing Eats

Apricot or Peach Bars

*Apricot or Peach Bars

2 cups flour   1 cup sugar
½ Tspn baking soda   ¾ cup chopped walnuts
1½ sticks margarine   1½ cups coconut
            2 cups jam*

1. heat oven to 350°
2. mix all ingredients except jam.
3. Press 3/4 of this mixture in baking pan
   or greased dish.
4. Spread jam over this, then sprinkle the
   remaining mixture on top of this. Bake
   25 - 30 minutes

2 cups flour
½ teaspoon baking soda
1½ sticks of margarine
1 cup sugar
¾ cup chopped walnuts
1½ cups coconut
2 cups jam - peach or
  apricot as preferred

1. Mix all ingredients
    except jam.
2. Press ¾ of mixture into baking pan or greased dish.
3. Spread jam over mixture.
4. Sprinkle remaining mixture on top.
5. Bake in preheated oven at 350° F for 25 to 30 minutes.
6. Cut to size.

Notes:

_____

_____

_____

_____

_____

_____

_____

_____

_____

_____

_____

_____

_____

Banana Bread

1¾ cup flour
1 Tablespoon baking powder
½ teaspoon salt
¾ cup sugar
½ cup butter
2 eggs
3 mashed ripe bananas

Optional
1 cup diced apples
1 cup walnuts
1 Tablespoon cinnamon
1 cup raisins

1. Preheat oven to 350° F. Grease 9x5-inch or 8x8-inch pan.
2. Mix flour, baking powder, salt, and set aside.
3. Beat sugar, butter, and eggs until light and fluffy.
4. Mix in bananas.
5. Add dry ingredients and stir until smooth.
6. Pour into pan.
7. Bake 50 to 60 minutes until firmly set.

Banana Bread

1¾ c. flour   ½ c. butter
1 tbsp. baking powder   2 eggs
½ tsp. salt   3 mashed ripe bananas
¾ c. sugar
Preheat 350°. Grease 9x5" or 8x8" pan. Mix flour, baking powder, salt & set aside. Beat sugar, butter, & eggs until light & fluffy. Mix in the bananas. Add dry ingred, & stir until smooth. Pour into pan & bake 50-60 min. (firmly set).

To reduce fat:
- substitute ½ c. apple butter for marj.
- use 1 whole egg & 1 egg white

Additions:
1 diced apple   1 tbsp. cinnamon
1 c. walnuts   1 c. raisins.

Notes:

Recipe: Banan Bread
From: _____ Makes: _____

1 3/4 Cups flour
2/3 Cup sugar
3 teaspoons baking powder
1/2 " " " baking soda
1/2 " " " salt
1/3 Cup margarine
1 Cup smashed bananas
2 eggs

BANANA BREAD

1 3/4 C flour
2/3 C Sugar
3 Tsp Baking Powder
1/2 Tsp SALT
1/4 Tsp Baking ~~Powder~~ Soda
1/3 cup marg. Crisco or butter Crisco
1 cup Ripe mashed Banana's (abt 3)
2 eggs

Optional
  Vanilla
  Cinnamon
  Walnuts
  Chocolate chip

Preheat oven 350° Grease Pans
Loaf well.

Into Large Bowl Combine:
Flour, Sugar, Baking Powder,
Soda, SALT. Cut in margine
and mix until it resembles coarse
crumbs.
→

BANANA BREAD

1 TEASP. BAKING POWDER

1/3 cup VEGETABLE oil
1 1/2 cups MASHED RIPE BANANAS
   (ABOUT 3 LARGE)
1/2 TEASP. VANILLA
3 EGGS
2 1/3 cups Bisquick BAKING MIX
1 cup sugar
1/2 Cup chopped NUTS

325° oven   1 Large Loaf
4 BABY Loaf Pans.

         MIX ALL TOGETHER
GREASE PANS.   Cook.

Add BANANA'S & EGGS. BEAT
with Electric mixer AT Low
Speed About 2 mins. Fold
In nuts and or Chocolate
Chips Bake 1 hour and 10 min
Approx. Allow Bread to
Cool 10 mins. Remove from
pan and Let cool
Completely on wire rack.

Carrot Pineapple Cake

Carrot Pineapple Cake

1 ½ c. flour
1 c. sugar
1 ½ tsp baking soda
1 ½ tsp cinnamon
½ tsp salt
2 - 4 oz. jars strained
    carrots
2/3 cup oil

2 eggs
½ tsp vanilla
1 8 oz. can crushed
    pineapple
2/3 c. coconut
½ c. raisins

Bake 40 to 45 min.
    at 350°

1½ cup flour
1 cup sugar
1½ teaspoon baking soda
1½ cup cinnamon
½ teaspoon salt
2 4-ounce jars of strained carrots
2/3 cups oil
2 eggs
½ teaspoon vanilla
1 8-ounce can crushed pineapple
2/3 cup coconut
½ cup raisins

Combine and bake at 350° F
for 40 to 45 minutes.

Notes:

Cranberry Nut Bread

2 cups flour
1 cup sugar
1½ teaspoon baking powder
1 teaspoon salt
½ teaspoon baking soda
¾ cup orange juice
1 well-beaten egg
2 Tablespoons shortening
1 Tablespoon grated orange peel
1 cup cranberries, coarsely chopped
½ cup chopped nuts

1. Preheat oven to 350° F.
2. Mix together flour, sugar, baking powder, salt, and baking soda.
3. Add orange juice, egg, shortening, and orange peel.
4. Mix well, stir in cranberries and nuts.
5. Grease – bottom only – of 9x5-inch loaf pan.
6. Bake 55 to 60 minutes or until tooth pick inserted in center comes out clean.
7. Cool thoroughly before serving.

Notes:

Cream Cheese Cake

Sugar Free Version

Crust:
1¼ cup graham cracker crumbs
2 Tablespoons soft margarine
2 teaspoon sugar substitute

Filling:
2 8-ounce packages cream cheese,
  brought to room temperature
2/3 cup of sugar substitute
3 eggs
1 teaspoon vanilla
1 pint sour cream

1. Mix crust ingredients together and press into spring form pan.
2. Mix cream cheese and sugar substitute with mixer.
3. Add 3 eggs, one at a time with electric mixer.
4. Fold in vanilla and sour cream.
5. Pour over crumb crust.
6. Bake at 375° F for 30 minutes and then leave in oven for 1 hour with oven turned off.

Cream cheese cake No Sugar

Mix
1 1/4 cup Graham Cracker
Crust
2 tbs. Soft Margarine
2 tsp Sugar Substitute
Press into Spring form pan

Allow: 2-8 oz packages cream
Cheese to come to room
temperature. With electric
beater beat in 2/3 cup of
sugar substitute.
Add 3 eggs one at a
time with Electric beater.
Fold in tsp Vanilla and
1 pint of sour Cream.
(over)

Pour over Crumbs.
Bake at 375° for 30
minutes and then leave
in oven for 1 hour with
oven turned off

Notes:

Cream Cheese Pie

1 graham cracker crust pie shell
1 8-ounce package of cream cheese
1/3 cup sugar
1 cup sour cream
2 teaspoons vanilla
1 8-ounce tub of whipped topping

1. Beat cream cheese until smooth.
2. Add sugar and mix.
3. Add sour cream and continue to mix together.
4. Add vanilla and beat.
5. Fold in whipped topping with a spoon.
6. Pour into pie crust.
7. Top as desired.
8. Refrigerate overnight.

Notes:
_____
_____
_____
_____
_____
_____
_____
_____
_____
_____

Cream Cheese Pound Cake

2 cups sugar
1 cup butter
8 ounces cream cheese
6 eggs
2 cups flour, sifted
2 teaspoon baking powder
Pinch of salt
1 teaspoon vanilla

1. Cream together sugar, butter, and cream cheese well.
2. Beat in eggs two at a time. Continue to mix well.
3. Add sifted flour, baking powder and salt. Mix well.
4. Add vanilla and mix well.
5. Pour into tube pan.
6. Bake at 350° F for 60 minutes or until tester comes out clean.

Notes:

Easter Bread

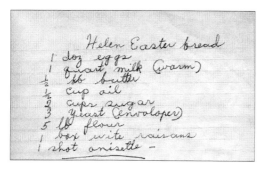

1 dozen eggs
1 quart milk, warm
½ pound butter
½ cup oil
2 cups sugar
3 envelope yeast
5 pounds flour
1 box white raisins
1 shot anisette

1. In a large bowl, combine 1 cup flour, sugar, salt, and yeast. Mix well.
2. Combine milk, butter, and anisette in a small saucepan. Heat until milk is warm and butter is softened but not melted.
3. Gradually add the milk and butter to the flour mixture, stirring constantly.
4. Add 2 eggs and ½ cup flour. Beat well. Repeat 4 times. Mixing well with each addition.
5. Add remaining flour, ½ cup at a time, stirring well after each addition.
6. When the dough has pulled together, turn it out onto a lightly floured surface and knead until smooth and elastic, about 8 to 10 minutes.
7. Lightly oil a large bowl(s). Place the dough in the bowl(s) and turn to coat with oil. Cover with a damp cloth. Let rise in a warm place until doubled in volume, about 1 hour.
8. Deflate dough and turn it out onto a lightly floured surface. Divide the dough into 6 equal size rounds; cover and let rest for 10 minutes. Roll each round into a long roll about 36 inches long and 1½-inches thick.
9. Take 2 long pieces of dough, form a loosely braided ring. Seal the ends of the ring together. Repeat until all dough is used.
10. Place loaves on a buttered baking sheet and cover loosely with a damp towel. Place loaf in a warm place and let rise until doubled in bulk, about 45 minutes. Brush risen loaf with melted butter.
11. Bake in oven preheated to 350° F until golden brown, about 30 minutes.

Dominick remembers a hardboiled egg
centered in the top of the pie.

Fried Bows

Fattigmands Bakkels from Ann Marie Barcello Ladrigan

3 egg yolks
1 whole egg
½ teaspoon salt
1 tablespoon rum flavoring
1 teaspoon vanilla
1 cup flour
¼ cup confectioners' sugar

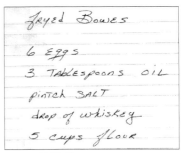

1. Heat deep frying fat, 2-inches deep, to 375° F.
2. Beat egg yolks, whole egg, and salt together until very stiff, about 10 minutes.
3. Blend in confectioners' sugar and flavoring thoroughly.
4. Add flour and mix.
5. Knead dough on well-floured, cloth-covered board until surface is blistered, about 7 minutes or so.
6. Divide dough in half. Roll out each half very thin.
7. With a pastry knife, cut dough into 4x2-inch diamonds.
8. Make 1-inch slit into the center of each diamond.
9. Draw a long point of the diamond through the slit and curl back in the opposite direction.
10. Fry until delicately browned, about ½ minute.
11. Drain.
12. Sprinkle with confectioners' sugar before serving.

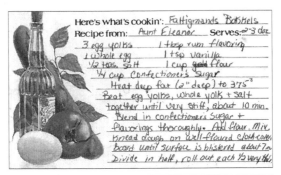

Fruit Cake – Elis Ilia

2 sticks butter soft
1½ cups sugar
4 eggs
1 teaspoon baking powder
1 teaspoon baking soda
1 teaspoon vanilla
3 cups flour
1 can pie filling, any flavor

1. In a large bowl, gently whisk together flour, sugar, baking powder, and baking soda. Create a well in the middle and add slightly beaten eggs and softened, not melted, butter.
2. Mix together, at this point turn mixture onto a slightly floured surface and work the mixture to form a soft dough. If dough is dry, then add an extra tablespoon of soft butter.
3. Wrap dough in plastic and refrigerate for 30 minutes. Remove from fridge and knead the dough on a lightly floured surface a couple of times to soften it. Roll out to 1/8-inch in thickness.
4. Transfer to ungreased 8-inch pie plate. Trim away extra dough.
5. Fill the shell with pie filling or jam.
6. Form extra dough into strips to create a lattice finish.
7. Bake in pre-heated oven at 350° F up to 35 minutes or until golden.

In Italy, many use homemade jams as pie filling.

Notes:

Fruit Cocktail Cake

1 lemon or yellow cake mix
1 package whipped topping
4 eggs
1 large can fruit cocktail and juice

1. Drain fruit cocktail and save the juice.
2. Mix cake mix, dream whip, 4 eggs, and 1 cup of fruit cocktail juice.
3. Add fruit and mix together.
4. Pour in tube pan.
5. Bake at 350° F for 60 minutes.

Fruit Cocktail Cake

1 lemon or yellow cake mix
1 package dream whip
4 eggs
1 large can fruit cocktail & juice

Drain fruit cocktail and save the juice.
Mix cake mix, dream whip, 4 eggs, and 1 cup juice from fruit.
Mix together.
Add fruit.

Notes:

Graham Cracker Cake

1 stick melted butter
2 cups graham cracker crumbs
1 cup walnuts
1 6-ounce bag of chocolate chips
1 1/3 cup coconut
1 can sweetened condensed milk

1. Mix together ingredients.
2. Bake at 350° F until tester comes out clean.

Graham Cracker Cake

1 stick melted butter
2 cups graham cracker crumbs
1 cup walnuts
1 6-oz bag chocolate chips
1 1/3 cup coconut
1 can sweetened condensed milk

bake : 350°

Notes:

La Pignolata Giallo

The Yellow Pignolata

1 tazza di farina bianga (1 cup white flour)
1 tazza di farina gialla (1 cup yellow flour)
1 uova (1 egg)
4 teaspoon baking powder
1 teaspoon baking soda
1 teaspoon salt
½ cup oil
1 cup latte (milk)

1. Combine ingredients and knead.
2. Roll into ¾-inch sticks.
3. Cut into ¼-inch balls.
4. Fry in deep oil.
5. Drain in colander.
6. Pour dark Karo syrup into frying pan.
7. Warm syrup and roll balls in syrup. Place on serving dish.
8. Add brightly red and green colored cherries to garnish like a Christmas tree.

Of all the dolci di Natale (sweets of Christmas), this was the long awaited wonder which meant the holiday had truly arrived. While Struffoli may be a Napoletana specialty, it is also popular in other regions of Italy. In Sicily, it is called Pignolata. In some areas, the little dough balls have a flatter shape.

Notes:

"My-Ti-Fine" Pie

Written by Lena Sottosanti

3 packages pudding for pie filling
3 packages sponge cakes
Cream topping of choice

1. Follow directions on box with 1½ cups water only.
2. Cut sponge cakes into slices.
3. Line bowl with cake slices and cover with pudding.
4. Turn bowl and repeat layers of cake slices and pudding.
5. Turn bowl again, repeat with layers of cake and pudding.
6. Finish with slices of cake.
7. Refrigerate overnight.
8. To serve, turn upside down and top with cream topping of choice.

Notes:

Pineapple Pudding Cake

1 box yellow cake mix and
   ingredients per instructions
1 box instant vanilla pudding mix and
   1½ cups milk
1 8-ounce package of cream cheese
1 15-ounce tub whipped topping
1 15-ounce can crushed pineapple
Cherries and chopped nuts

Pan Size: 12" x 17"

1. Bake one Duncan Hines yellow cake mix. Let cake cool.

2. Mix one package Instant Vanilla Pudding with 1 1/2 cups milk. Beat for about two minutes. Set aside and let thicken while preparing rest of icing.

3. Mix one 6 oz. package of Philadelphia Cream Cheese and one 15 oz. container of Cool Whip. Beat until smooth. Add vanilla pudding to this mixture and beat for about two minutes.

4. Spread on cake.

5. Drain a 15 oz. can of crushed pineapples and sprinkle over cake.

6. Place cherries on cake and sprinkle chopped nuts on top.

7. Keep cake refrigerated.

1. Bake yellow cake mix in a 12x17-inch pan. Let cool.
2. Mix instant pudding with 1½ cups milk. Beat for 2 minutes. Set aside to thicken.
3. Mix cream cheese with whipped topping and beat until smooth.
4. Add vanilla pudding to mixture and beat for about 2 minutes.
5. Spread mixture on cake.
6. Drain can of crushed pineapple and sprinkle over cake.
7. Place cherries on cake and sprinkle with chopped nuts.
8. Refrigerate until served.

Notes:

_____

_____

_____

_____

_____

_____

_____

_____

_____

_____

pan size 12" x 17

1 Bake one Duncan Hines yellow cake mix let cool.

2 Mix 1 Package instant Vanilla Pudding with 1½ cups milk Preparing rest of icing.

3 Mix one 8 oz. Package cream cheese and one 15 oz. Container of Cool Wip. Beat until smooth. add vanilla pudding to this mixture and beat for about two minutes.

4 Spread on cake.

5 Drain a 15 oz. Can crushed pineapple and sprinkle over cake.

6 Pace cherries on cake and Sprinkle chopped nuts on top.

7 Keep cake refrigerated

Rice Pudding

RICE PUDDING   OVEN 325°
3 SLIGHTLY BEATEN EGGS
2 CUPS MILK
1½ CUPS COOKED RICE
½ CUP SUGAR
1 TSP VANILLA
½ TSP SALT
CINNAMON
½ CUP RAISINS (OPTIONAL)

~OVER~

3 slightly beaten eggs
2 cups milk
1½ cups cooked rice
½ cup sugar
1 teaspoon vanilla
½ teaspoon salt
Cinnamon
½ cup raisins (optional)

1. Preheat oven to 350° F.
2. In a bowl, combine all ingredients except cinnamon.
3. Bake in 10x6x2-inch dish at 350° F for 25 minutes.
4. Stir and sprinkle with cinnamon.
5. Continue baking until knife comes out clean, 20 to 25 minutes.

IN BOWL, COMBINE ALL INGREDIENTS
EXCEPT CINNAMON. BAKE IN 10X6X2
DISH AT 350°FOR 25 MINUTES.
STIR- SPRINKLE WITH CINNAMON-
CONTINUE BAKING TIL KNIFE COMES
OUT CLEAN (20 TO 25 MINUTES)

rice Pudding
3 eggs beaten
1 cup milk
light cream
sugar
1 tsp vanilla
1 cup cooked rice
raisins
tsp nutmeg
bake oven 350
55 or 65 min

Notes:

Ricotta Cake

1 box of yellow cake mix and
   ingredients per instructions
1 pound ricotta cheese
1 cup of sugar
4 eggs
1 teaspoon vanilla

1. Mix the cake as directed.
2. Combine remaining ingredients.
3. Pour cake mixture into a 9x13-inch greased pan.
4. Carefully spoon cheese mixture over the top.
5. Bake at 350° F for 60 minutes.

<u>Notes:</u>

_____
_____
_____
_____
_____
_____
_____
_____
_____
_____
_____
_____

Ricotta Pie

Ann Marie Barcello Ladrigan

Dough:
¾ cups butter
1½ cups flour
¼ cup sugar
1 teaspoon baking powder
2 eggs

Filling:
1 cup ricotta cheese
½ cup peeled wheat (grano)
·½ cup sugar
2 eggs
¼ cup chopped citron
¼ cup chopped cherries

RECIPE FOR: Ricotta Pie — Pizza Ricotta Pie

Dough   350° Bake
¾ cup butter   ¼ cup sugar   1 hr or till golden
1½ cups flour   2 eggs
1 tsp baking powder

Filling
1 cup ricotta   2 eggs
½ cup peeled wheat (grano)   ¼ cup chopped citron
½ cup sugar   ⅛ cup chopped cherries

Soak peeled wheat 2-3 days. Then cook in water for 2-3 hrs. Mix everything together. And fill. Take remaining crust and cut into strips and place criss-cross across top of pie. Brush with beaten egg yolk.

1. Soak peeled wheat for 2 to 3 days.
2. Cook soaked wheat in water for 2 to 3 hours.
3. Make dough for crust. Roll out and place in greased pie pan.
4. Mix all filling ingredients together and fill crust.
5. Take remaining crust and cut into strips and place in criss-cross pattern across top of pie.
6. Bake at 350° F for 60 minutes.

Notes:

Scalletta

Scalette

10 eggs
1 tablespoon Crisco
1 pinch salt
2 shots of whisky
beat eggs soli rossi uno brango brango
anisette   add flour as much as it
takes   irabant aslo bene et rest
fry them, them roll in honey or
Conf. sugar

10 eggs
1 tablespoon shortening
1 pinch salt
2 shots of whiskey
Anisette
Flour, as much as the mixture can take
Honey or confectioners' sugar

1.   Soli rossi uno brango, or beat the egg yolks (or reds).
2.   Add in melted shortening and anisette.
3.   Add flour, in as much as it takes.
4.   Add in remaining ingredients as you go.
5.   Make sure the dough is not too sticky.
6.   Roll out dough into 10-inch long by ½-inch thick segments.
7.   Wrap dough around a wooden-spoon handle 4 or 5 times to make a twist.
8.   Slip out the spoon and wrap the twist with a loop.
9.   Fry them.
10.   Roll in honey or confectioners' sugar.

It is said, a Christmas without Scalletta is no Christmas. These cookies are lots of fun to make.

Notes:

_____
_____
_____
_____
_____
_____
_____
_____
_____
_____

Sour Cream Cake

Ann Marie Barcello Ladrigan

2 sticks butter
2 cups sugar
3 eggs
1 pint sour cream
3 cups flour
1 teaspoon baking soda

Topping
Equal parts of brown sugar,
sugar, and walnuts

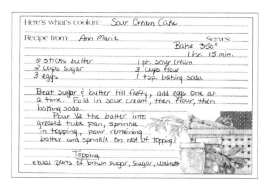

Here's what's cookin': Sour Cream Cake

Recipe from: Ann Marie   Serves
                      Bake 350°
                              1 hr. 15 min.
2 sticks butter   1 pt. sour cream
2 cups sugar   3 cups flour
3 eggs   1 tsp. baking soda

Beat sugar & butter till fluffy, add eggs one at
a time. Fold in sour cream, then flour, then
baking soda.
       Pour ½ the batter into
greased tube pan, sprinkle
in topping, pour remaining
batter and sprinkle on rest of topping.

       Topping
Equal parts of brown sugar, sugar, walnuts

1. Beat sugar and butter until fluffy.
2. Add eggs one at a time.
3. Fold in sour cream, then flour, then baking soda.
4. Pour half of the batter into greased tube pan.
5. Sprinkle in topping.
6. Pour remaining batter into pan and sprinkle on the rest of the topping.
7. Bake at 350° F for 75 minutes.

Notes:

Sweet Easter Pie

Frine Liffredo

2 cups rice, cooked in water and cooled
½ teaspoon salt
1 cup sugar
6 eggs
1 pound ricotta cheese
1 teaspoon vanilla
1 pie crust, at least 2-inches deep

1. In a large bowl, beat the ricotta cheese, eggs, and sugar until smooth. Stir in the vanilla extract. Fold in the cooled rice.
2. Fill pie crust. Extra dough can be used as lattice across the top.
3. Bake at 450° F for 10 minutes.
4. Lower temperature to 350° F and bake an additional 50 minutes. Pie should be lightly browned on top and may be slightly jiggly toward center. Will set up when cool.
5. Let cool completely. Serve chilled or room temperature.

Notes:

Eleonora's Amazing Eats

Taralli a la Eleonora

2 pounds of all-purpose flour, approximately 6 cups
½ yeast cake or 1 package active dry yeast (2¼ teaspoons or 8 grams)
2 ounces of cooking oil (approximately ¼ cup)
2 cups lukewarm water
3 eggs (room temperature)
1 teaspoon sugar
Pinch of salt
Pinch of fennel seeds
Coarse black pepper to taste

1. In a medium bowl, stir yeast with water. Let stand for 10 minutes, allowing it to get foamy.
2. In another bowl, combine flour and salt.
3. Add eggs and oil to yeast mixture. Mix together to combine.
4. Add liquid mixture to flour mixture.
5. Add fennel seeds.
6. Knead until mixture becomes a soft, smooth elastic dough.
7. Gather dough, place on a well-floured wooden board.
8. Shape into a log.
9. Cover with wrap and dishcloth, place in warm spot. Allow dough to rest until doubled in size; up to 2 hours.
10. Bring a large pot of water to boil.
11. With a sharp knife, slice dough into 18 equal parts. More segments if you want smaller pieces.
12. Roll each piece into a rope. Form into a ring or desired shape. Press ends firmly together.
13. Plunge taralli in boiling water; 3 to 4 at a time ensuring ample room.
14. Once they come to the top, turn them over in the water and continue to boil for 1 minute. The entire boiling process should take less than 2 minutes.
15. Remove with slotted spoon. Place on cooling rack to drain.
16. Repeat process until all the taralli have been boiled.
17. Slit all round taralli.
18. Place boiled taralli directly on oven grates.
19. Set oven rack one below the center and bake at 350° F for 45-60 minutes or until golden brown.

Taralli a la Grace

12 eggs
6 teaspoons sugar
12 Tablespoons oil
2 handfuls of self-rising flour and regular flour
A little baking powder
A little whiskey

1. Mix ingredients together.
2. Role into ropes and twist into desired shapes.
3. Boil twice.
4. Bake in oven at 450° F.
5. After 10 minutes, lower oven to 350° F and cook for several more minutes.
6. Lots of Luck!

Notes:

Walnut Torte

1 cup flour
3 Tablespoon brown sugar
¼ pound margarine
1 teaspoon vanilla extract
1 cup chopped walnuts
1 8-ounce package cream cheese
1 cup confectioners' sugar
3 cups whipped topping
2 3¼-ounce packages chocolate pudding
3 cups milk

1. Mix flour, brown sugar, margarine, and vanilla.
2. Add ½ cup chopped walnuts.
3. Press into 9x13-inch pan.
4. Bake 375° F for 10 minutes until lightly browned. Let cool.
5. Blend cream cheese, confectioners' sugar, and 1 cup of whipped topping.
6. Spread on crust.
7. Cook pudding with milk until thick.
8. Spread over cream cheese layer while still hot.
9. Chill.
10. Top with 2 cups of whipped topping or whipped cream.
11. Sprinkle with remaining ½ cup walnuts.

Walnut Torte
(Serves 14-16)

1 Cup flour   1 8 oz. package cream cheese
3 Tablespoons brown sugar   1 Cup confectioners sugar
1/4 pound margarine   3 Cups whipped topping
1 Teasp. vanilla extract   2 3¼ oz pkgs. chocolate pudding
1 Cup chopped walnuts   3 Cups milk

        Mix flour, brown sugar, margarine and vanilla. Add
1/2 cup chopped walnuts. Press into 9x13 pan. Bake 375º
for 10 minutes until lightly browned. Cool.
        Blend cream cheese, confectioners sugar and 1 cup
of whipped topping (we used IGA brand from Bethel Food
Market). Spread over crust.
        Cook pudding with milk until thick. Spread over
cream cheese layer while still hot.
        Chill. Top with 2 cups of whipped topping (or
whipped cream). Sprinkle with remaining 1/2 cup walnuts.

Wheat Pie

"To Elinor... Love Helen"

12 eggs
3 pounds ricotta cheese
2 teaspoons vanilla
3 cups milk
3 cups wheat
2 cups sugar
Pie or pastry dough of choice

1. Prepare wheat in a large saucepan. Bring water to a boil and pour in wheat and allow to boil 40 minutes.
2. While wheat is cooking, beat eggs in a large bowl and gradually add 1 cup sugar to eggs. Mix in ricotta and vanilla.
3. When wheat is ready, drain in a colander and rinse well with warm water.
4. Preheat oven to 350° F.
5. Line a 9-inch pie pan with pastry or pie crust. Cut remaining pastry into strips for tops of pie(s). Cover with pastry strips to form a lattice. Crimp edges of dough together.
6. Bake until crust is golden brown.
7. Sprinkle with 1 tablespoon sugar and cool at room temperature.
8. Chill overnight before serving.
9. Refrigerate any leftovers.

Notes:

_____

_____

_____

_____

_____

_____

_____

Zeppole

Brian Watson

1 cup warm water
1 teaspoon active dry yeast
1 tablespoon sugar
1 teaspoon salt
2 cups all-purpose flour
Chopped anchovies, optional
Sugar, tomato sauce, or gravy as desired for topping

1. Mix yeast, sugar, salt and water. Let stand a few minutes and stir to dissolve.
2. Combine flour, yeast mixture and olive oil until dough is sticky. Cover with plastic wrap and let rise for 90 minuets in a warm place.
3. Portion, shape into balls generally 4-inches in diameter.
4. Add chopped anchovies, when shaping, if desired.
5. Fry in 350° F oil.
6. In the best spirit of grandma, add sugar, tomato sauce, or enjoy plain.

Notes:

_____

_____

_____

_____

_____

_____

_____

_____

_____

_____

Zucchini Muffins

2 large eggs, beaten
½ cup melted butter
¼ cup milk
1½ cups flour
½ cup sugar
2 teaspoon baking powder
½ teaspoon baking soda
½ teaspoon salt
½ teaspoon cinnamon
2 cups grated fresh zucchini
Nuts, raisins, or cranberries (optional)

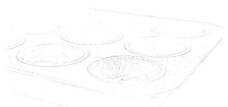

1. Mix dry ingredients in bowl.
2. Cut in melted butter.
3. Mix in zucchini.
4. Mix in eggs and milk.
5. Toss with fork.
6. Bake in oven at 350° F for 20 minutes.
7. Add nuts and/or raisins while warm.

Zucchini Muffins
Mix dry ingredients in bowl
1½ Cups flour
½ cup sugar
2 teaspoon baking powder
½ teaspoon baking soda
½ teaspoon salt
½ teaspoon Cinnamon
cut in butter throw in
zucchini mix egg &
milk toss with fork
oven 350 · 20 mins
add nuts raisins

Notes:

_____
_____
_____
_____
_____
_____
_____

Accounts of Eleonora

My Sister
Angelina Annunziata Moccia Barcello

Eleonora possessed a caring, strong, and vibrant personality.

She would make a dessert delicacy called "Fritelle" or "bowties." A delicious deep fried "bowtie" pastry made infrequently, yet often for special occasions. For instance, a wedding shower.

Our sister, Theresa, and her husband, Rudy, had 12 children who especially enjoyed this delicacy, but the quantity was never quite enough to satisfy their large family.

Eleonora was good at making practical jokes. SOOOO...

She made up a batch of the "bowties" -- a whole bushelful! She purposely presented the entire bushelful to Rudy, my husband's brother and my brother-in-law, because he said he would never get enough of his fill of them! Keep in mind the family was composed of two parents and 12 children.

When she presented this delicacy to him, she used this Italian (dialect) expression which was, "buota e schiatta," that translates to EAT AND HAVE YOUR FILL! In my memories, it resounds as a fond expression of her playfulness and one of her special characteristics of sharing her love of cooking and her spirit of sharing and generosity.

Great Aunt Angie

Moccia siblings and their spouses

Paul	Joe	Tommas	Rudy
Eleonora	*Angie*	*Mary*	*Theresa*

Aioli Anchovy & Pasta

Brian Watson

I thoroughly enjoy crafting in the kitchen. Something I believe my grandmother Eleonora gifted me. Even now, I continue the effort of recreating her amazing eats. Here is one of my fondest memories of her.

It was 1990 and the World Wide Web was only a proposal. Information was passed on by "old school" means. Yes, by books or person-to-person; if you can image that. I was in my early 20s and my grandmother was a spry 74; by now it was clear she was not one for writing things down.

On any given Sunday, for our weekly family visits, she might make Aioli Anchovy and Pasta. She would emphasize with her lingering Italian accent, "I make Aioli Aioli special for you." Often noting that I was the only one who liked it.

Seemed only fitting this was the first recipe of hers I attempted to replicate. With my dad as guide and my recollection as assistant, I gave it go. It was good. Real good actually. Just...not quite right. So, I tried again. And again. And... exhaustingly... Again! Still something was missing.

I turned to the master herself. "I show you," she said and a tutorial followed. We were in her realm, the eat-in-kitchen of 63-B Taylor Street in Bethel, CT, where gatherings over good food and, "Mangia," was often ordered.

Missing something small, I knew I had to watch closely. The instinctual cook appeared and operated on her ingredients like a skilled surgeon. In a truly rare moment, she called out the steps with precision. She announced, "Add a cup of water to anchovy." Then... It Happened.

She stopped, seized the measuring cup with her full, yet, nimble fingers, and... dipped it into the pasta pot while it was still boiling and in a flash, dumped it into the sauce pan.

"Wait. Wait! What? Hold on, Grandma! What was that?"

She looked over with a smirk and a furrow of her brow, and matter-of-factly stated, "Cup 'a water!" Then glanced at the pot of boiling pasta like it was the faucet; indicating clearly...where you are supposed to go for water.

And that was it. My quest for the complete Aioli Anchovy and Pasta recipe was a success with the simple, yet magical, cup of starchy water.

*Eleonora and Paul,
January 1966*

Creating Cavatelli
Ann Marie Barcello Ladrigan

The cavatelli recipe included in this book is from Aunt Eleonor's instructions. The ingredients are right on, however, there are a bunch of tricks that I am not allowed to write down. If I do, Aunt Eleonor will haunt me from the grave.

The story begins at her house in Bethel. Aunt Eleonor had been in this country for over 60 years and still had her heavy Italian accent. She was funny without meaning to be funny... and sometimes she did mean to be funny. With only a third-grade education, she was one of the smartest, most practical women I have ever known – and a fabulous cook.

She could grow amazing vegetable out of sand... I'll never forget the huge zucchini hanging about 15 feet up in a tree because she tossed some seeds down from the second story window of their Wright Street apartment in Stamford. She never worried about animals getting in her garden because, as she would say, "theya gotta eatta too!"

So, I'm at her house one day and I'm grabbing her hand to try and figure out the amounts of the ingredients because she never measured anything. We got the dough made and it was resting and she told me the most important procedure out of the whole recipe and I started writing it down.

She smacked my hand! I reacted with, "What was that for?"

She scolded, "Don'ta you write-a that-a down-a!"

"Why not?"

She snapped, "It'sa none of nobody's-a business!"

So I've never dared write it down. I have taught my son, Sean, how to make cavatelli and he knows the secret. He makes it for his godmother, Aunt Fran, for Christmas. You may have never seen it because she runs and hides it, like a priceless treasure, before anyone finds out.

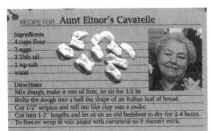

If you want to learn the secret, I can teach you how to make it. In the meantime, "it's-a none of nobody's business!!"

***

Even for this book Ann Marie did not complete the cavatelli instructions. She left them to Eleonora's granddaughter, Denise, who completed the recipe's secrets from her own cavatelli creating experiences with her grandmother.

The Amazing Eleonora

Ann Marie Barcello Ladrigan

It was tough to get all those recipes out of Aunt Eleonor!

I loved that she made me come to her house and show me exactly how to do it "lika dis." I would have to constantly grab her hand and dump it into a measuring cup to have some idea of what HER "handaful" was. I can still feel the sting of her smacking my hand as I would go to write down the most important part of the process.

Not an ingredient...the process which made all the difference between really good and that.... *oh-my-God-this-is-amazing*.

Aunt Eleonor may not have had a lengthy formal education, she was one of the smartest women I have ever known.....smart, funny, and practical with an ability to laugh at herself.

I refuse to cut corners when making the pizza gana which takes, all told, a full week. I will not use pre-made crust. Mainly because she will haunt me if I do!

Bow ties are my daddy's favorite! Aunt Eleanor would show up at our house with a wicker hamper basket filled with these treats covered with a dish towel. She handed them to my dad, who would hide them in our pantry because he didn't want to share. I remember sneaking into the pantry and climbing on to the dryer to reach into the basket to steal a bow tie. I was sure to wipe the evidence of powdered sugar off my shirt before going back to the dinner table. When I made them for my dad this year, he grumbled that they were just, "OK" and that... "Aunt Eleonor made them much lighter."

"Dammit Daddy...You're never going to have her fried bows again. I did my best!"

That woman--that amazing woman-- ingrained in me, subtly, the importance of teaching hands-on, and that emailing a recipe is a poor substitute for learning hands-on with the master. And as we worked together, we laughed, we cried, we shared stories, and she set me straight on some things that I was confused about because she wasn't afraid to tell me the truth about family. Not judgmental, just the truth so that I felt better.

Some may have seen her as tough, yet I knew her as a mischievous imp.

I loved every deep smile groove in her face and I miss her terribly to this day.

Spun Up
Greg Watson

In the mid- to late-80s, when I came home from college on break my grandmother had a to-do list of painting projects. With each break, I would give a room, or the stairwell, or a hallway a fresh coat of color.

Good thing, a completed project was a guaranteed way to get something wonderful to eat. She knew everyone's favorite treat. For me, she would always make the best pizza fritte (fried dough). I would top it with a hearty helping of cinnamon and sugar. It was truly a treat - that amazing sweet, crispy crunch of hot dough and sugar. There is nothing like it, even to this very day.

While fried dough was my favorite food, it didn't accompany my fondest memories. Those were of the family visits for cookies and coffee -- typically close to Easter and Christmas. Sure, she always had her list of chores that we had to complete before we were granted treats. It was what followed that was the most fun. I loved it when my dad would tell us to throw her cookies out the window and try to hit the birds with them because they were "too hard" and "terrible." He would continue the taunting by saying that her coffee was really bad, too.

Of course, everything she made was fantastic. My dad just really liked getting her all spun up. And when she was spun up, that wooden spoon of hers was whipped out like a magic wand. She would get all sorts of huffy and flabbergasted. Then, when her frustration was beyond words, she would shake that wooden spoon at us as if to cast a spell for good behavior. We would all laugh at her and her empty gestures, because the spoon was nothing more than the magician's cooking wand.

Special time together in June 1995

In the end, you could tell she loved the teasing even if she didn't admit it. After it all, there was always a smile, a hearty laugh, a kiss goodbye, and a loving farewell wave.

Until next time, Grandma.

Eleonora's Amazing Eats

Where the Magic Happened

Renee Watson

I truly love this picture of my dad, Thomas, and "Mama," as I called her. The expressions on both their faces are simply priceless! It is even more fitting that they are in the kitchen because that is where all the magic happened.

As for my special memories... I'd say it starts with Meatballs! There was always a pot of meatballs and gravy simmering on top of the wood burning stove. Every Sunday, after church, there were meatballs. Ah, the savory smell of simmering meatballs and gravy filled Mama's entire home.

Her garden is another memory that makes my heart happy. I have the fondest memories of walking up and down the sun-blocking rows of vegetables. Snapping fresh green beans off their vines and popping cherry tomatoes in my mouth like they were candy. Looking back, I can honestly say my love of fresh produce came from all those summers snacking in her garden.

Thanks, Mama!

My mom, Camille, Mama, and me on an afternoon picnic, about 1980.

A Love of Rare Intensity

Camille Watson

Mama was my inspiration for how to cook and how to live. We spent many hours together, with and without my "babies." My fondest memories are the visits after church on Sunday. There was always a pot of gravy on the stove simmering. Usually full of meatballs but sometimes sausage, pork ribs or chops, and/or braciole. We often stayed for lunch, especially if she had water for pasta boiling on the stove.

Other times there was pizza fritte (fried dough) or a frittata (scrambled eggs and the vegetables of the day), and, oh, how I loved to find her making pasta fagioli. It is still my favorite soup. She made a fabulous chicken soup, as well.

Then there were all those times I stopped over after school with the kids. It was a pleasure to be there. You felt so welcome. She would scurry around making hot cocoa or setting out glasses of milk for her grandchildren and offering up her specialty of the day. I loved to sit there and chat with her over fresh coffee about all the family news. She was so proud of them all.

I was an eager learner having married very young. I still find myself in awe of the talent she had for making the simplest of food utterly delicious. She would take fresh vegetables from the garden Papa loved and they both tended it all summer long. Her eggplant parmigiana is still the best I have ever had. If you never tasted her stuffed squash flowers, then you have missed a delicacy beyond words. Fried green tomatoes in the Fall were something to look forward to; they were oh so scrumptious. It was wonderful to see Jeff or Renee pick fresh string beans, peas, or cucumbers right off the vine and eat them with delight.

I loved to replicate her cakes and casseroles. While she tried to teach me how to make her famous cookies, I found the whole process a bit too intricate and I simply couldn't find the interest to make them properly.

Once she asked what I would do when she was no longer here. I said, "We will miss you very much." And, that we do.

Mama loved her family with a rare intensity, which I always admired. To me it seemed food was her way to show that. She was truly remarkable.

A Bouquet of Memories

Joyce Nuzzo Taborsak

My Nani was the kindest person I have ever known. She was so full of love and laughter; no matter the situation, she had a ready smile and an open heart.

I have so many fond memories of her that it is difficult to choose just one; so instead I choose to gather them like a bouquet.

My Nani is the smell of fresh baked bread, the grassy aroma of snapped green beans, the cool breeze on a hot summer night out in front of her little house.

She is the crunch of sprinkles on her famous White Cookies, the sound of crickets in the evenings, and the swish swish of yarn being crocheted into a bedspread.

Nani is walks to the corner store, visits to old friends in Stamford, and endless supplies of Clairol products.

She is hot coffee and biscotti, General Hospital, and freshly made pasta.

My Nani is all this and much more; too many memories to share just one.

So I give you these impressions that live in my head and in my heart for the rest of my life.

Amore Sempre
Regina Barcello

When my boys Andrew and Jeremy were little, preschool aged, so mid- to late-1980s, we used to visit Aunt Eleonor two to three times a week, stopping by while on the way to do errands or on the way back from errands. She always had a cup of coffee percolating, or dripping, or on the stove, or in the French press. I thought it was interesting she used all different kinds of coffee pots. And there seemed to always be homemade cookies available, especially at Christmas (biscotti, anisette cookies, thumbprint cookies), or zucchini quiche, or her apple cake. And if there wasn't that, there was her manaste soup or she would run out to the garden and pick something to throw in a pot.

My Andrew, as a toddler, was vegetable-averse. But give him Aunt Eleonor's Minestrone or Manaste soup and he ate with gusto. One of my favorites, and I thought was an odd combination until I tasted it, was her peas and eggs. I think the process was to sauté onions, throw on some tomato sauce, a handful of fresh peas until heated and 'frying' some eggs on top of all that. I can never make it taste anything like she did!

And then there was her garden. Their home in Bethel was situated on a hill and they dug that garden into the hillside working around lots of rocks and stones to get it level and the soil tilled. She was able to get a lot of vegetables out of that small garden. She had a rain barrel under the downspout of her gutters, she added Miracle Gro to that water, which she used to water the garden. Tomatoes, beans, squash flowers - all went into her cooking. She even used to go mushroom hunting, I think in the woods around her home, and add that to her soups.

We visited her for years in her Bethel home and even after she moved into that cute red 'retirement' apartment. It was during our visits that the kids and I got to know my husband's Moccia/Watson side of the family: Eleonor's daughter Martha, her daughters Joyce and Christine would stop by occasionally, her daughter-law Camille and her two kids Renee and Jeff. And I would occasionally bump into her sons Dominick and Tommy there.

It was touching to see how she loved her family and showed it by her cooking.

My boys still have fond memories of that coffee and her goodies, and grew up into fine cooks themselves, partly from seeing her 'throw something together.'

Saluti Aunt Eleonor!
Il nostro amore sempre
(our love always)!

Eleonora, Regina, and Michael.

The Best
Theresa Barcello Metzgar

I have so many fond memories of Aunt Eleonor.

She was truly our grandmother in place of Grandma Moccia, who I only have vague memories of as a very little girl visiting her in Newtown.

I am Eleonor's sister, Theresa, and her husband Rudy's oldest child of 12. Our parents would pile us into the car to go visit Aunt Eleonor and Uncle Paul on Wright Street in Stamford, and then in Bethel years later.

She was the best cook and always had food going on the stove and managed to feed us, be it zeppole on St. Joseph's feast day or she would visit us with a basketful of bow ties for my dad!

She was a joy to be around!

Sometimes us kids would be shooed off to the movies with our older cousins as chaperones, so the adults could talk.

I remember her Christmas time tea dainty cookies especially. She must have made them by the dozens!

There always seemed to be a pot of gravy going on her stove and lots of vegetables growing in her garden that she always would walk you outside to admire the abundance.

She was truly the best!

Numero Uno
Michael Barcello

Some of my earliest and happiest memories are of Aunt Eleonor. As a child, and an adult, I learned from her and was inspired by her. She was always active and always ready with a laugh. Her bounty of kindness and love was expressed in many ways, the most memorable being with food. If she liked you, you ate well... and she liked everyone. If you were visiting Eleonor, you better show up with an appetite.

I recall many times when the kitchen table at Wright Street was converted into a near-magical production line of raw ingredients being transformed into <u>amazing</u> food. A pinch of this, a dash of that. No measuring cups ever used!!! This food was created **by feel.**

Even at an early age, barely tall enough to reach the table, I was allowed to help. Not pretend help. Really help. I recall being propped up on a chair and using fork tines to seal the edges of the homemade raviolis.

Ravioli, zeppole, Christmas cookies, eggplant parm. You name it, hers was numero uno! For me, all Italian food is ranked on the Aunt Eleonor Scale. The range is "Not even close to Aunt Eleonor's" to the highly coveted "Almost as good as Aunt Eleonor's." Before you dare to ask, there is no such category as "Better than Aunt Eleonor's," because that is the culinary science equivalent of traveling at the speed of light: Theoretically impossible and nobody has ever come close.

Aunt Eleonor was an inspiration in and out of the kitchen. I am so pleased that a part of her love will live on thru this book.

Eleonora with Michael at his Christening.

Sometimes the real heroes in life don't wear capes, they wear aprons.

Salute Dearest Eleonor

Nephew and godson
Migueluche (Michael) Barcello

Eleonora's Amazing Eats

Indelible Eleonora

Denise Ann Watson

My grandmother Eleonora was an extraordinarily magical individual. Her effervescent personality and her incredible cooking made her kitchen the hub for gatherings of family and long-time friends. Those of us fortunate to be part of her special circle were blessed to have personally enjoyed Eleonora-made eats. Sunday mornings to annual holiday celebrations, Eleonora's amazing eats were ideal for any — and every — occasion.

It is not surprising that there are really only a few stories of Eleonora contained within these pages. In creating this splendid assemblage of recipes, even I was thoroughly challenged trying to recount the memories and defining my grandmother for others. With her, every occasion was special, every moment was filled with love, and every second worthy of remembrance.

In short, my grandmother was simple times, Sundays, and family; percolating coffee, smirky expressions, home-grown produce, and holidays; and laughter, love, huge hugs, warmth, and... good food.

Over many years, her friends and family endeavored to pen and preserve her recipes and capture her incredible essence in the process. She saved every effort they made, as their time together was — without a doubt — immensely meaningful to her. I can say with absolute certainty that her heart and her love are in every word, every recipe, and every stained note of this book. Eleonora is, perhaps, the definition of indelible.

May the smells of making her amazing eats in your kitchen envelop you and fill you and your family with the joy and happiness we know to be Eleonora. For her family and friends, the smells of her cooking are the lingering impressions of her eternal love.

In my best essence of Eleonora, I say with great Italian gusto, "Mangia! Mangia!"

Make. Eat. Be Merry.

Con tutto il mio amore (with all my love), Gran'ma!

Denise

Eleonora with her great granddaughter Kailyn, Christmas 1999.

Index

citron 79
cloves 13, 18, 25, 58, 60
coconut 39, 47, 61, 64, 73
cornflakes 8, 39
  Cornflake Macaroons 39
cranberries 65, 88
  Cranberry Nut Muffins 65
cream 34
  heavy cream 34
  cream topping 75
cube steaks 19

D
dates 40
  Date Bars 40

E
Easter 10, 11, 12, 69, 82
  Easter Bread 69
  Easter Macaroni Pie 10
  Easter Pie: Pizza Chiena (Pizza Gana) 11
  Easter Pie: Pizza Rustica 12
  Sweet Easter Pie 82
egg 9, 10, 11, 12, 16, 17, 18, 19, 24, 25,
  26, 27, 28, 30, 31, 33, 34, 35, 39, 40,
  45, 46, 48, 49, 55, 58, 59, 60, 62, 64,
  66, 68, 69, 71, 72, 77, 78, 79, 80, 81,
  82, 83, 84, 86, 88, 96, 98
  egg white 14, 43
  egg yolk 11, 37, 38, 54, 55, 70, 80
eggplant 14, 96, 100
escarole 13
  Escarole with Beans 13

F
fennel seeds 83
flour 7, 9, 11, 12, 14, 17, 23, 24, 30, 31,
  33, 34, 35, 36, 37, 38, 40, 41, 43, 45,
  46, 48, 49, 50, 52, 53, 55, 57, 58, 59,
  60, 61, 62, 64, 65, 68, 69, 70, 71, 74,
  79, 80, 81, 83, 84, 85, 87, 88
fried 14, 23, 70, 90, 93, 94, 86
  Fried Blossoms 14
  Fried Bows 70, 90, 93
  fried dough 23, 94, 96
fruit cocktail 72

G
garlic 5, 6, 13, 15, 18, 20, 25
graham cracker 47, 66, 67, 73
  Graham Cracker Cake 73
gravy 15, 19, 23, 87, 95, 96, 99
  brown gravy 19
  Gravies & Sauces 15

H
Ham 16
  Ham & Broccoli Casserole 16

J
jam 38, 61, 71
jelly 38

K
Karo Syrup 49, 74

L
lemon 14, 35, 72

M
macaroni 10
  Easter Macaroni Pie 10
Manicotti 17
maple syrup 23
margarine 30, 31, 33, 39, 45, 46, 47, 55,
  61, 66, 85
milk 16, 27, 45, 46, 47, 58, 60, 69, 73,
  74, 76, 77, 85, 86, 88, 96
  sweetened condensed milk 47, 73
  buttermilk 58, 59, 60
mint 14
meatballs 15, 18, 25, 95, 96
  Meatballs 18
molasses 41
  Molasses Butter Balls 41
mushrooms 8, 27, 98

N
nutmeg 17, 48, 57, 58, 60
nuts 36, 38, 40, 43, 47, 48, 50, 52, 55,
  58, 60,6 5, 73, 76, 81, 85, 88

O
oil 5, 6, 7, 9, 13, 14, 15, 17, 18, 19, 20,
  21, 22, 23, 24, 25, 28, 49, 53, 54, 59,

Made in the USA
Lexington, KY
28 October 2018